Kate Edna Negley

The Negley Cook Book

Kate Edna Negley

The Negley Cook Book

ISBN/EAN: 9783744792073

Printed in Europe, USA, Canada, Australia, Japan

Cover: Foto ©Andreas Hilbeck / pixelio.de

More available books at **www.hansebooks.com**

THE NEGLEY COOK BOOK,

Compiled and Edited by
MISS KATE EDNA NEGLEY,
Teacher in the McKelvy School Kitchen, - - - Pittsburg, Pa.

THE INDEX PRESS, PITTSBURG, PA.

1898.

Entered according to Act of Congress, in the year 1898,
by Miss Kate Edna Negley,
in the office of the Librarian of Congress, at Washington.

"All human history attests
That happiness for man—the hungry sinner—
Since Eve ate apples, much depends on dinner!"
—Byron.

This book
is dedicated to my
Mother,
who possesses rare merit
in the
Art of Cookery.

INDEX.

Things Necessary to Know,	9
Soups,	13
Oysters,	17
Fish,	20
Meats,	23
Warmed-Over Meats,	27
Potatoes,	29
Vegetables,	33
Batters,	39
Cereals,	44
Stewed Fruits,	47
Candies,	50
Eggs,	57
Cheese,	62
Custards,	67
Puddings,	73
Pudding Sauces,	80
Salads,	85
Salad Dressing,	91
Cakes,	94
Icings,	107
Beverages,	111
Bread and Doughs,	113
Small Cakes,	120
Pies,	129
Cold Meats and Sauces,	136
Desserts, Ice Creams and Sherbets,	142
Jellies, Pickles and Relishes,	149
INVALID COOKERY,	154
Vegetables to Serve with Meats,	176
Menus,	177
How and When to Do Things,	179
The Table and Serving,	182

Things Necessary to Know.

1. Flour, butter, baking powder and sugar are measured rounding by the spoonful—rounding means the same on top as in the bottom.
2. Salt, pepper, soda, cream of tartar and spices are measured level by the spoonful.
3. tsp. stands for teaspoonful.
    tbsp. stands for tablespoonful.
    c. stands for cupful.
    spk. stands for speck.
    hp. stands for heaped.
4. 3 tsp. equals 1 tbsp. 4 c. flour equals 1 lb. 4 level or two rounding tbsp. equals ½ c. 2 c. butter equals 1 lb. 2 c. sugar equals 1 lb. 3 c. meal equals 1 lb. 2 c. meat equals 1 lb. 1 hp. tbsp. butter equals 2 oz. 1 hp. tbsp. sugar equals 1 oz. 1 tbsp. liquid equals ½ oz.
5. Always sift flour before measuring.
6. A cupful means full to the top. A scant cupful, is within ¼ inch from the top.
7. ½ pint cup is the standard measuring cup.
8. Dredge means to sprinkle.
9. Seared means to brown without water.
10. Skewers are pins used for roasts, etc.
11. Baste means to take the water or whatever it is cooking in and pour over the food.
12. Wash meats by taking a cloth wet in cold water and wipe good; putting meats in water extracts the juice.
13. Uniform means the same thickness.

14. Cleanse fish with a cloth wet in salted water and scrape well.

15. The flesh of good fresh fish is firm and hard.

16. Onions are scalded to make them tender, and remove some of the strength.

17. Deep fat means enough fat to float the food.

18. Wash parsley by holding it in cold water, then shaking it gently on the hand.

19. Chop parsley by twisting it together and then cut fine.

20. Garnish means to decorate.

21. Stock is the water in which either fish, meat, vegetables, etc., have been cooked.

22. Wash oysters by putting them in a colander, and pouring cold water over them.

23. Temperature is the right heat for cooking.

24. Poultry seasoning is a mixture of herbs.

25. Simmering is when the bottom of the pan is covered with little bubbles.

26. A pinch is as much as you can take between your thumb and first finger.

27. Spk. is what you can put on the point of a teaspoon.

28. Onion juice is gotten by grating the onion.

29. For lemon juice you squeeze the lemon.

30. Save all pieces of bread; dry, roll and sift them; keep them in a glass jar or tin box. You will always need bread crumbs.

31. Always scrub vegetables with a small brush kept for that purpose.

32. Cook vegetables in salted water, using 1 tsp. salt to 1 qt. water. Also meats.

33. In cooking cereals of any kind, always cook them over carefully, and remove any foreign substance.

35. Wash rice in three or four waters, rubbing it well between the hands.

36. In cooking dried fruits, never put in the sugar until about five minutes before done, as by long cooking it loses its sweetness.

37. Fried foods should be drained on brown paper.

38. Never put fried foods on top of each other.
39. Wash eggs as soon as they come from the store, as you do not know what disease germ is lurking on the shell.
40. Keep eggs in a cool place.
41. A fresh egg sinks in a pan of cold water; a stale egg rises to the top.
42. The yolk may be kept fresh by covering it with cold water; it will keep for several days if the film is not broken.
43. Keep milk covered.
44. Change the water on butter milk every day, it will keep in a good condition, use cold water.
45. Cheese should be kept covered.
46. Use tough meat from the round for beef tea as it contains more juice.
47. The following seasonings may be used with warmed over meats:

Cayenne, chopped parsley, onion juice, celery sauce, pickles, curry, mint, mustard, lemon juice, vinegar, horseradish, tomatoes, herbs and nutmeg.

48. In making soups put your meat in cold water, as it draws out juice.
49. Scald raisins before seeding.
50. In using moulds for steaming, always grease them. If for jellies, etc., rinse with cold water but do not dry them.
51. Bread should be thoroughly cooked and kept in a tin box.
52. Pan for bread should be 8 in. long and 4½ in. wide, 4 in. deep.
53. Grease pans for biscuits and bread.
54. Never put the butter in the oven to melt, heat your bowl with hot water, dry, and then put in your butter.
55. Beat whites of eggs until dry, not just stiff.
56. Fruit should be floured before adding to the mixture to prevent them sinking to the bottom.
57. Cakes should be baked according to their composition.
58. Test with a straw, when it comes out clean the cake is done.
59. Always mix pastry with a knife.

60. Do not grease your pans for pies.

61. Pies should be baked $\frac{1}{2}$ to $\frac{3}{4}$ of an hour.

62. Handle pastry as little as possible.

63. Do not add flavoring to custards and puddings until they are cool; that is if it can be done, as it requires twice the amount, it loses its strength.

64. Never allow the cork to remain out of an extract bottle, it is made with alcohol and will evaporate.

65. Never cook foods containing acids in tin, as it will eat the tin, which is poisonous.

66. Soak all soiled dishes in cold water.

67. Cover boiled meats with a plate as soon as done to prevent it from becoming discolored.

68. Mix cornstarch with a little cold water before adding to boiling liquids.

69. Sprinkle a little flour on cakes before icing, as it prevents the icing from spreading.

SOUPS.

BOUILLON.

6 lb shin bone with meat,
2 qts. cold water, 1 tbsp. herbs.

Wash meat, cut in small pieces, put in sauce pan with the water and herbs tied in a bag, simmer five hrs., strain and season, serve with croutons.

CROUTONS.

Butter slices of bread, cut in squares (small) and brown in the oven.

CONSOMME.

2 qts. chicken stock,
1 small onion, 1 small carrot, 1 small turnip,
1 tbsp. parsley, 2 tbsp. butter,
Salt and pepper.

Chop the vegetables and fry in the butter, until brown, add to the stock and simmer several hours; if not the chicken stock, use 2 lbs. of shin beef, put on in cold water and when it comes to the boil add the vegetables, and simmer the same as for chicken stock, strain, serve clear, or with the whites of two hard cooked eggs, cut in small pieces.

CREAM OF BISQUE SOUP.

2 c. tomatoes, 1 qt. milk,
1 tbsp. cornstarch, 2 tbsp. butter,
Salt and pepper,
Pinch soda.

Cook the tomatoes until soft, heat the milk in double boiler, melt butter, add cornstarch, and part of the milk, let boil five min., pour all into the boiler, add soda to the tomatoes, and when the gas has all passed off strain into the boiling milk; to prevent curdling remove the top part of the boiler from the fire, adding the tomatoes.

CORN SOUP.

Split the grains of 1 doz. ears of corn (or 1 can), and scrape, cook the cobs in enough water to cover them five min., strain, keeping 1 qt. Blend 1 tbsp. flour, and 1 tbsp. butter, add slowly 1 qt. boiling milk, then the corn, pour all into the corn water, season, and let boil twenty min., if can corn is used cook ten min., either strain or leave the grains in; serve hot.

OYSTER SOUP.

1 qt. oysters, 1 pt. milk,
1 pt. oyster liquor and water,
1 tbsp. flour, tbsp. butter,
1 onion, salt and pepper.

Heat the milk in double boiler, cut onion in large pieces and cook with the water and liquor five min., strain into the milk, blend flour with a little cold milk, pour into the hot milk, cook 15 min., stirring often, add oysters, salt, pepper and butter, cook until the oysters curl on the edges; serve hot.

TOMATO SOUP.

1 can tomatoes, 1 pt. water or stock,
1 tbsp. sugar, 3 tsp. salt.
4 cloves, 4 pepper corns.
1 tbsp. butter, 1 tbsp. chopped onion.
1 tbsp. chopped parsley, 2 tbsp. flour.

Cook the tomatoes, cloves, pepper, salt, sugar and water 15 min., cook the onion and parsley in butter until brown(do not burn), add flour and then the tomatoes; boil 10 min., strain; serve with croutons.

VEGETABLE SOUP.

2 lb. shin bone, 1-4 lb beef,
2 small onions, 2 small carrots,
2 small turnips, 4 potatoes,
1 bunch celery, 1 c. tomatoes,
1-2 c. cabbage, 1 tsp. sugar,
2 tsp. salt, 1 qt. cold water.

Put the salt, sugar, water and meat on to boil, melt 1 tbsp. butter, and cook the vegetables (excepting potatoes and cabbage) in it until brown, add to the stock, also tomatoes and cabbage and season, simmer three hrs., 1 hr. before serving par-boil the potatoes five min., cut in dice, a thickening may be made by adding 2 tbsp. flour to the browned vegetables, thin with a little of the soup before adding.

CLAM SOUP.

Cook thirty clams chopped fine, in 2 qts. cold water, using the juice also, fry a large piece of bacon (1-4 lb., cut in small pieces), and in it cook two large onions, chopped fine, and a little parsley, add 3 tbsp. flour, thin with a little of the broth, add seasoning, cook hard one hr. Take from the fire and add 1 pt. hot milk, in which have been broken 4 eggs; remember not to cook again.

MULLAGATAWNY SOUP.

1 calf's head, 4 qts. cold water,
2 onions, 4 cloves, 1-8 tsp. pepper,
1 tbsp. curry powder, juice of 1 lemon,
2 tsp. salt, 1 tsp. sugar.

Cook the calf's head and water and cloves 10 min., fry the chopped onion in a little beef drippings, add to the stock, mix curry powder, salt pepper and sugar, thin with a little of the broth, add to the stock also the lemon juice. Simmer until the meat is tender, remove the head, cut the meat in small pieces, and return to the soup, take the brains, cut up and mix with them 1 raw egg and a little bread crumbs, roll in balls, and drop in the soup when ready to serve.

CREAM PEA SOUP.

1 can peas, 1 qt. stock.
1 c. milk, 2 tbsp. butter,
2 tbsp. flour, 1 onion,
1 tbsp. chopped parsley,
Salt and pepper.

Cook the onion, peas and stock together 15 min., mash through a sieve, blend flour and butter together, thin with a little of the soup, add to the rest of the soup also cream and seasoning; cook 3 min., add parsley, and serve with croutons.

MOCK TURTLE SOUP.

Cover 1 calf's head with 1 gal. of water, cook 3 hrs. or until the flesh will slip from the bones; take out, select enough of the fatty portions to fill a c. and set aside to cool. Remove brains to a saucer also set aside. Chop the rest of the meat with the tongue, fine; season with salt, pepper, powdered marjorem and thyme, 1 tsp. ground cloves, mace and ½ tsp. of allspice and 1 grated nutmeg, return to the soup and cook 1-2 hour longer; 5 min. before lifting throw in "Forced Balls," made by rubbing the yolks of 5 hard cooked eggs to a paste, adding the brains to moisten, a little butter and 2 eggs, beaten very light, mix well, flour the hands, and make the mixture into balls the size of a very small egg, add to the soup, also the whites chopped in small pieces, 1 tbsp. browned flour, rub smooth in a little cold water, and 1-2 glass of sherry wine and juice 1 lemon.

OYSTERS.

SCALLOPED OYSTERS.

To prepare oysters for cooking take up each oyster separately in the fingers and remove all bits of shell. Place in a colander and rinse with cold water. The juice may be strained through a cloth or fine strainer. The oysters should be placed in layers with seasoned crumbs between each layer. The oysters if used in shells are cut into small pieces.

1 pt. oysters, 2 c. crumbs.
3 tbsp. butter, salt and pepper.
Oyster juice or milk.

Prepare the melted butter and crumbs. Use half the crumbs in layers between the oysters and reserve the other half for the top of the dish. Add either oyster juice or milk sufficient to moisten. Cayenne is a good seasoning used with black pepper. Bake in a hot oven until the crumbs are a delicate brown.

FRIED OYSTERS.

Select large oysters, put them into a colander and pour cold water over them to wash, wipe with a cloth. Remove carefully small pieces of shell. Season with salt and pepper. Roll in fine bread crumbs (which have been dried and sifted) then in beaten egg and again in crumbs, or roll in corn meal or dip them in a batter. When the fat is at the right temperature put in the oysters a few at a time and cook until browned, (about three min).

MACARONI AND OYSTERS.

Cook 1 pt. macaroni in boiling water twenty min., pour off water and add 1 pt. milk, cook until milk is absorbed. Butter a baking dish, put in 1-3 of the macaroni, 1-2 pt. raw oysters, 1 slice of bacon cut fine, salt and cayenne pepper (a very little salt as the bacon may have sufficient), then half the macaroni, 1-2 pt. of oysters and 1 slice of bacon, put the remainder of the macaroni as a crust on top, season and moisten well with oyster liquor or milk.

OYSTER FRITTERS.

Wash 1 pt. oysters, chop fine and add to a batter made from 1 pt. milk, 2 c. flour or a little more, 1 tsp. baking powder, salt and pepper. Fry a light brown.

SOYER CUTLETS.

Chop fine 1 lb. of lean veal,
Chop fine 1 pt. raw oysters,
Chop fine 2 tbsp. veal suet.

Soak 4 tbsp. soft bread crumbs in enough oyster liquor to cover them; mix all together and add yolks of 2 eggs; season with salt and pepper, make into small cakes, roll in fine bread crumbs, beaten egg and again in crumbs, fry in butter slowly. You will find them rather soft, but if you do not make the cakes too large you will have no trouble.

LITTLE PIGS IN BLANKETS.

Wash large oysters and put between two large slices of bacon cut thin, pin with tooth picks. Cook in hot oven until the bacon is crisp. Serve hot.

OYSTER SOUP.

1 pt. oysters, 2 tbsp. butter,
1 pt. milk, 1 tsp. salt,
1 tbsp. flour, pinch pepper.

Put milk in top part of double boiler, cook with it one onion, cut in slice, and a little celery. Cook for 15 to 20 min.

Heat the oyster liquor and 1 c. hot water. Melt the butter, add the flour, and a little of the hot milk, cook five min., add the rest of the milk and strain into the oyster liquor, add seasoning and oysters, cook until the oysters are heated.

OYSTER PATTIES.

1 pt. small oysters,
1 pt. cream, 1 large tsp. flour,
Salt and pepper.

Let the cream come to a boil, mix the flour with a little cold milk, add to the cream, season, let boil 5 min., while cooking, let the oysters come to a boil in their own liquor, skim carefully, drain off all the liquor; add the oysters to the sauce, boil up at once, fill the shells and serve. This is enough for eighteen shells.

SHELLS.

1 qt. pastry flour,
1 c. ice water.
Scant 1-4 tsp. salt,
2 c. butter.

Wash the butter well in cold water, cut in four pieces, and put on ice until hard, mix the flour and salt, take one piece of butter and rub into the flour with the tips of the fingers, be careful it is not soft, add the water, using a knife to stir, sprinkle a little flour on the board, roll out the dough, take another piece of butter, cut in small pieces and put on the dough, fold and roll out again, add the third piece, fold, roll and add the last, then fold and roll about eight times, then roll the thickness desired, 1-2 in. and cut, do not remove the centres until baked, the oven must not be too hot at first or they will burn, if too cold will melt and not raise. Should bake thirty to forty min.

FISH.

BOILED FISH.

To boil nicely, without breaking, fish should be of uniform thickness. Lay a fish on a plate in the centre of a cloth and tie the corners loosely together; boil hard 5 min., then cook slowly for 15 min. to each pound. Serve with egg sauce.

BROILED FISH.

Broil the oily fish, such as shad, herring, blue fish, etc. Grease a wire broiler. Cut off tail, head, fins, remove eyes, etc., lay the fish, cook over red hot coals, turning often; when done the flesh separates easily from the bone; you can then remove the back bone without any trouble. Serve with brown sauce.

FRIED FISH.

Fish may be skinned, boned and cut in small pieces or fried whole if desired; wash and dry, roll in flour, season with salt and pepper, or you may roll it the same as for fried oysters, cook in deep fat. Cooking slowly in a small amount is much better. Serve drawn butter sauce.

BAKED FISH.

Wash, wipe and dry the fish, rub with salt, fill with stuffing and sew the edges together, cut gashes in each side across the fish, not very deep, and put strips of bacon into them; dredge with flour and bake without water in a hot oven. Baste with the fat every 10 min. after the flour has browned. Instead of the fat you can cook the fish in milk enough to cover the bottom of the pan, do not use flour. The milk keeps the fish moist and browns as nicely as flour. The fish is cooked when the flesh is firm and on being touched separates easily from the bone. Serve with tomato sauce.

STUFFING FOR BAKED FISH.

1 c. soft bread crumbs,
1-4 tsp. salt, 1 tsp. chopped parsley,
1-8 tsp. white pepper, 1 tsp. lemon juice,
1 tsp. chopped onion (scalded), 4 level tbsp. butter,
1 tsp. chopped pickle, milk or egg to moisten.

SALT FISH BALLS.

4 medium sized potatoes,
1 c. shredded salt fish,
2 tsp. butter, 1 egg,
Pinch pepper.

Pare the potatoes and cook until soft enough to mash; drain very dry and add butter, seasoning and beaten egg. If you use the shredded fish soak it in cold water about 10 min., if not wash and shred the fish; cook in water about 20 min., drain well and add to the mashed potatoes, beat and shape into balls and cook in deep fat until brown. Any kind of cold fish may be used in these balls.

CREAMED CODFISH.

1 tbsp. butter, 1 tbsp. flour,
1-8 tsp. white pepper, 1 pt. hot milk,
1-2 pt. shredded codfish.

Melt the butter, add flour, pepper and slowly the hot milk, cook five min., add fish, well drained; if the fish is not salty enough add a little, pour in the center of a hot dish and put a border of mashed potatoes, sprinkle chopped parsley over the fish, serve hot.

FISH ON TOAST.

1 tbsp. butter, 1 tbsp. flour,
1-4 tsp. salt, pinch pepper,
1 c. milk, 1 egg,
2 tbsp. cold cooked fish.

Melt the butter, add flour, seasoning and milk, beat well and cook three min., add fish and cook two min. longer, remove from the fire, add beaten egg, pour over dry or softened toast. Serve garnished with hard cooked eggs. A nice breakfast dish.

SCALLOPED SALMON.

1 can salmon or pt. of fresh salmon,
2 c. soft bread crumbs,
1-2 tsp. salt, 1-8 tsp. white pepper.
2 tbsp. butter.

Melt butter and pour over crumbs, mix well, put 1-3 of the crumbs in a buttered baking dish, sprinkle in 1-2 the salmon, a little seasoning, half of the remainder of the crumbs, the rest of the fish, seasoning and make a crust with the rest of the crumbs, moisten with fish stock(water in which the fish has been cooked) or water and bake until a golden brown. Serve with any kind of sauce.

MEATS.

ROAST MEATS.

Trim and skewer into shape and lay in pan, place in the oven until seared, turn that it will not burn but be seared on both sides. Dredge with flour, salt and pepper and pour on a little water. For a small roast allow 10 min. to each lb., a large roast 15 min. Baste often. Serve with a gravy.

BROILED STEAK OR CHOPS.

The steak should be from 1-2 to 1 1-4 in. thick, wipe it, cut off any fat, grease a broiler and lay the meat upon it; hold over a clear fire, count ten slowly and turn, so on until done; 1-2 in. steak will require from 3 to 5 min., if rare, well done 8 to 10 min., same for chops. 1 1-4 in. steak 8 to 10 min., rare, and 15 to 20 well done, season, and serve with butter or Maitre deHotel, butter, or mushroom sauce.

PAN BROILED STEAK OR CHOPS.

Cut off fat; heat a frying pan, when you throw in a little cold water it hisses, lay in the meat, counting ten, turn and continue counting and turning for 5 min. if liked rare; 7 min. well done. Brown the fat of chops by turning them on edges. Serve as the above.

BAKED STEAK OR HEART.

1 tbsp. dried bread crumbs,
1-4 tsp. salt, 1-4 tsp. poultry seasoning,
1 tsp. chopped onion,
Pinch pepper,
Water or milk to moisten.

Buy a calf's heart, wash well in cold water and cut out the

veins and arteries, mix the crumbs, seasoning, scald the onion, and add to the crumbs, *** heart or steak. Brown the heart or steak in a little fat that an onion has been cooked in, put in a dish, cover with water; bake 1 hr., basting often. Serve with gravy made from the stock in which the meat was cooked.

VEAL LOAF.

3 lbs. veal, chopped fine.
1-4 lb. pork, lean, chopped fine.
8 soda crackers.
2 tbsp. milk.
2 eggs.
2 tsp. salt.
1-8 tsp. pepper.
1 tsp. poultry seasoning.

Mix all together, be sure and roll the crackers fine, shape into a loaf, put in a greased pan, put a small piece of butter on top, when browned add water, cook about 3 hrs., basting often.

BEEF OLIVES.

1 1-2 lb. lean beef off the round.
3 tbsp. fine bread crumbs.
1-4 tsp. poultry seasoning.
1 tsp. salt.
Pinch pepper.
1-4 lb fat pork.
1 1-2 pts. boiling water.
Flour.

Cut any fat from the meat; chop fine and add to the crumbs and seasoning, cut the meat into pieces 3 in. in width and 4 in. long and season, spread the stuffing on each piece, roll and tie with string; roll in flour. Try the fat from the pork, remove pork and brown olives, when brown put in a covered sauce pan and pour on the water, put 1 tbsp. flour in the pan in which the olives were cooked; thin with a little of the water; pour all into the sauce pan, and simmer for 2 hrs.

VEAL POT-PIE.

1 tsp. salt, pinch cayenne pepper,
2 lbs stewing veal, 2 qts. water,
1 onion, 2 potatoes (if desired),
1 c. cream or milk,
2 tbsp. butter, 2 tbsp. flour.

Cut the veal in small pieces, (put a plate in the bottom of the stew pan so that the veal will not burn) and put with the water and onion in a stew pan, cook slowly for about 2 hrs., add salt and pepper, and potatoes cut in dice, cook ½ hr. longer; melt butter, add flour, and pour in cream, cook for 5 min., stirring all the time, add to the stew, pour over biscuits made from

1 qt. flour, 1 tsp. salt,
4 tsp. Rumford baking powder,
2 hp. tbsp. butter and lard
1½ c. milk or cold water.

VEAL BIRDS.

Slice of veal from the loin, cut very thin, remove the bone, skin and fat and pound until ¼ in. thick; cut into pieces 3 in. long and 2 in. wide; chop the fat that was cut off with a small piece of bacon, add half as much fine bread crumbs as you have meat, season with salt, pepper and poultry seasoning.

Moisten the filling with water, egg or milk; spread the mixture on the slices of meat, roll, tie with a string, roll in flour, and brown in a little butter, then put in a sauce-pan and cover with milk or cream, and simmer until tender, remove strings and serve on toast, garnished with pieces of lemon.

BREADED LAMB CHOPS.

Trim, wipe and season chops, roll in fine bread crumbs, beaten egg and again in crumbs, fry slowly in a little butter until a golden brown. Serve garnished with peas.

YORKSHIRE PUDDING FOR ROAST BEEF.

1 pt. milk, 4 eggs.
1 c. flour, 1 tsp. salt.

Mix quickly, pour off fat from top of gravy, leaving gravy in the pan to prevent sticking, pour in batter, bake ½ hr., if able to leave the roast in so the dripping from the meat can fall on the pudding it is better so, baste meat with the fat poured off the gravy. Serve with the roast cut in squares.

SWEET BREADS WITH MUSHROOMS.

Parboil sweetbreads until tender, allowing eight medium ones to one can mushrooms, drain, remove skin, and cut in small pieces, stew mushrooms in their own liquor 1 hr., to the sweetbreads add 1 c. cream, salt pepper and 1 tbsp. butter; when tender and ready to serve add mushrooms, and if desired 2 tbsp. wine. Sweetbreads broiled and served with peas makes a very dainty dish. Brains may be used instead of sweetbreads; is just as nice and much cheaper.

Warmed-Over Meats.

CREAMED MUTTON.

Cut thin a few slices from a cold cooked leg of mutton, sprinkle with salt, pepper and poultry seasoning; fry them in 2 tbsp. butter; lift, stir into the pan in which the meat was cooked, 1 tbsp. flour, 1 tbsp. lemon juice, and thin with 1 c. gravy or stock; simmer 5 min., pour over meat and serve immediately.

LAMBS' FRY.

Boil 1 lb. lambs' fry in 3 pts. of water, 20 min., drain, and wipe dry. Mix some fine bread crumbs, salt, pepper and parsley together. Dip the fry first in bread crumbs, then in beaten egg, and again in crumbs. Fry in butter 5 min.; brown on both sides. Serve very hot on a paphin on a steak platter. Garnish with parsley.

SAUSAGE ROLLS.

Make a dough as for baking powder biscuits; roll and cut into pieces 4 inches wide and 8 inches long. Take a sausage and put in the dough, roll up, press the ends together, and bake ½ hr. in a hot oven.

HASH.

Cut 2 c. meat in dice or small pieces, put into a frying pan with enough water to cover it; add 2 medium sized potatoes cut in cubes, 1 large onion chopped fine, and 1 small carrot cut fine; simmer for ½ hr. Blend 1 tbsp. butter and 1 tbsp. Worcestershire sauce, season, and serve on toast cut in squares.

LEFT-OVER ROAST BEEF.

Cut the meat into thin slices, dip in beaten egg, and brown in butter. Serve on a steak platter, garnished with parsley and hard cooked eggs, cut in quarters.

STEWED KIDNEYS.

Wash a beef kidney, remove all fat and cut in small pieces, put on in 1 pt. water and ½ tsp. salt. Cook hard from 15 to 20 min.; pour off that water and cover and let simmer several hours. Ten minutes before serving make a thickening of 2 tbsp. of browned flour and cold water; stir thin into the kidney, also 1 hp. tbsp. butter, salt, pepper, pinch mustard, and if desired, ½ c. sherry wine. This is a nice dish served with fried mush.

MEAT PUFFS.

To one bowl of finely chopped cold cooked meat add 1 c. bread crumbs, yolks of 2 eggs, beaten stiff, a little onion juice, seasoning, parsley, and a little herbs, if liked; beat the whites stiff and fold in. If not moistened enough add a little gravy or stock. Roll in balls, and fry in a bath of boiling hot fat. Serve on a hot steak platter, garnished with parsley.

POTATOES.

MASHED POTATOES.

Cook six potatoes in boiling water until soft. Drain and mash well. Add ½ tsp. salt, pinch of pepper, 1 tbsp. butter and hot milk sufficient to moisten. Beat well.

FRENCH FRIED POTATOES.

Cut potatoes in quarters, fry in a bath of fat until brown; drain; season with salt.

CELERY POTATOES.

Chop fine six large raw potatoes and a small bunch of celery. Heat a frying pan until hot; put in 1 tbsp. of butter, and 1 tbsp. lard or drippings; put in potatoes. Cook slowly until browned well on one side; turn and brown on other. They should only be turned once. They may be cooked the same way with onions, using 2 large onions to 6 potatoes.

CREAMED POTATOES, No. 1.

6 cold cooked potatoes,
1 c. milk, ½ tbsp. butter,
¼ tsp. salt, pinch pepper,
1 tbsp. chopped parsley.

Melt the butter, add seasoning, and pour on the milk, stirring all the time; cook five min. Butter baking dish, put in potatoes, pour on sauce, and sprinkle the parsley on top. Brown in a hot oven.

CREAMED POTATOES, No. 2.

6 large potatoes, 1 c. milk.
1 tsp. salt, 2 tbsp. butter.
Pinch pepper, 2 tbsp. chopped parsley.

Cut potatoes into dice, put with the milk in a double boiler, cook until they have absorbed nearly all the milk. Add butter and seasoning; cook five min. longer. Add the parsley. Serve hot.

BAKED POTATOES.

Bake potatoes until soft; cut open long-wise; remove potatoes without breaking the shell; mash well, season with salt, pepper and a little butter. You may mix grated cheese, or beat the white of 1 egg until stiff, fold into the potato, put back in shell, cover with the yolk, brown in a hot oven. One egg will be enough for about six potatoes.

EGGED POTATOES.

Beat the yolks of two eggs until creamy; soften 1 tbsp. butter, (holding over steam of tea-kettle), mix 1 tbsp. parsley and 1 tbsp. lemon juice with the yolks; add to the butter; stir all together, heating over steam. Cut 1 pt. cold cooked potatoes into dice, heat by putting into ½ c. hot milk. Mix all together, and serve hot. Garnish with parsley.

LYONNAISE POTATOES.

1 pt. cold boiled potatoes.
1 tbsp. onion juice.
1 hp. tbsp. butter.
Salt and pepper, 1 tbsp. chopped parsley.

Cut the potatoes into cubes. Fry the butter and onion until yellow. Add the potatoes, and stir with a fork until the potatoes have absorbed all the butter. Be careful not to break them. Add the parsley and serve hot. Sweet potatoes may be cooked in the same way as the white.

POTATO PUFF.

Mash five potatoes and beat until light; add 1 c. milk, 2 eggs and a good-sized lump of butter; season; beat well; bake in a buttered pudding dish until a golden brown, in a hot oven.

ESCALLOPED POTATOES.

1 hp. tbsp. butter, 2 tbsp. flour.
½ c. cream, ½ c. stock.
2 eggs, 2 tbsp. cheese (if desired).
Salt and pepper.
4 cold boiled potatoes.

Melt the butter and flour, thin with cream and stock; cook five minutes; pour into the eggs well beaten, also cheese, season, put in a buttered baking dish a little of this mixture, then the potatoes, sliced, continue so on until the dish is filled; sprinkle buttered crumbs on top. Bake until brown.

POTATO BALLS.

2 c. flour, 2 eggs.
1 c. milk, 6 potatoes (grated while warm).
½ tsp. salt.

Separate the eggs, beat the yolks until creamy, add milk, salt and flour; beat well; also potatoes, lastly fold in the whites beaten stiff. Fry in a bath of boiling hot fat. Drop by the spoonful, and they will form into balls. When a yellow-brown, remove from the fat.

VEGETABLES.

BEETS.

Scrub beets without breaking the roots. Boil until they can be easily pierced with a skewer. Pour off the water and hold under cold water, and the skin will peel off without any trouble. Serve with salt, pepper and butter, or vinegar or milk sauce.

ONIONS.

Peel onions, holding under cold water. Put on in cold water, and when they come to a boil cook ten minutes. Change the water three times, in last let them cook until tender. It usually takes them ¾ to 1 hour. Drain, season with salt, pepper and butter, enough milk to cover. Cook five minutes longer.

STEWED CABBAGE.

Cut cabbage as you would for slaw, but not so fine; put into a sauce pan with boiling water; do not cover with a lid; cook until tender—about 1 hour. Drain, serve with salt, pepper, butter and milk, or white sauce. Cauliflower is cooked the same way, only tie it in a bag so it will not fall to pieces.

SPINACH.

Wash spinach in several waters, after picking from the stems. Cook in boiling salted water about 15 minutes; drain well. Melt 1 tbsp. butter in a frying pan. When hot put in 1 tbsp. flour and spinach (½ pk.) season with salt and pepper. Add ½ c. soft bread crumbs and two eggs, well beaten. Cook two minutes. Serve on steak platter; garnish with hard cooked eggs, or serve in baskets made from slices of bread 2 in. thick, dipped in egg and browned in oven—cut out center.

CELERY.

1 large bunch of celery,
1 pt. water in which the celery was cooked,
1 c. milk, 2 hp. tbsp. flour,
2 hp. tbsp. butter, salt and pepper.

Cook celery until tender, drain, keep the water. Melt butter, add flour, seasoning, and hot milk. Cook five minutes, stirring all the time. Then pour on water, add celery, re-heat, and serve.

BAKED TOMATOES.

Skin tomatoes by putting them in boiling water about three minutes; remove the cores, make a filling, ½ c. soft or dried bread crumbs, 1 tbsp. butter, salt and pepper, a little onion juice; moisten with milk, egg or water, mix all together, fill centers of tomatoes, on each place a small piece of butter, dredge with salt, pepper and flour. Cook from twenty minutes to half hour. Baste often. This amount will fill ½ doz. large tomatoes.

PARSNIP FRITTERS.

Scrape off a thin skin, and cook parsnips until tender; drain, mash, season with salt and pepper, and to about three parsnips ½ tbsp. butter, 1 egg beaten a little, ½ tbsp. flour, mix well, and pat into flat cakes; dip in flour; fry brown in butter.

CORN PUDDING.

1 can, or 1 pt. corn, 2 eggs,
1 pt. milk, 2 tbsp. butter,
Salt and pepper.

Beat eggs, add milk, seasoning, corn and 1 tbsp. butter. Butter a baking dish, pour all in; cut the other tbsp. butter into small pieces and put on top. Bake in a hot oven about ¾ hour.

CARROTS.

Scrub and scrape off a very thin skin. Cut into dice, cook in boiling salted water until soft. Serve with white sauce.

BAKED BEANS.

1 qt. beans, 1 lb. salt pork.
3 onions, 1 tbsp. butter.
1 tbsp. carrots, ½ bay leaf.
8 whole peppers, 2 cloves.
1 tbsp. flour, 2 c. tomatoes.
1 tbsp. salt, 1 tbsp. sugar.

Soak the beans in cold water 4 hours, drain, add fresh cold water, 2 of the onions whole, and the pork cooked until tender. Remove onions and pork, drain beans. Melt the butter in a sauce pan, and add the other onion and carrots chopped fine, cloves, bay leaf, whole peppers and cook ten minutes. Add flour, and thin with the tomatoes. Cook five minutes longer, season with the salt and sugar, strain, add beans to the sauce, put in a pudding dish or pan. Lay the pork in the center and bake 1 hr.

FRIED TOMATOES.

Cut tomatoes in slices, without skinning, dip in flour, or fine bread crumbs, fry, put on a hot platter, make a gravy by putting a little flour in the fryings in which the tomatoes were cooked, season, thin with milk, cook a few min., and pour over tomatoes. Serve hot.

FRIED CABBAGE.

Chop cabbage fine, wash in cold salted water, drain, fry in pork fat, lamb fat, or drippings for 20 minutes, covered; then remove the cover, and let cook until tender and brown.

CREAMED TOMATOES.

Cut tomatoes in slices, not too thick; lay in a buttered baking dish; rub the yolks of 2 hard cooked eggs with 1 tbsp. weak vinegar, and 1 tbsp. butter melted, 1 tbsp. sugar, pinch salt, cayenne and mustard; stir until smooth. Pour over this mixture 2 raw eggs and ½ c. milk. Pour over the tomatoes; cut the whites of the hard cooked eggs fine, sprinkle on top; bake ½ hr. in a hot oven. Serve at once.

ASPARAGUS.

Wash the asparagus, and scrape the tough end; boil in salted water until tender; lay on buttered toast; make a dressing by melting 1 tbsp. butter; add ½ tbsp. flour; thin with 1 c. hot milk, boil 5 min.; season; pour over the asparagus.

FRIED HOMINY.

Cook the hominy in boiling water until tender; drain, melt 1 tbsp. butter in a frying pan; put in hominy (1 c.), and cook until brown. Season. One-fourth c. cream may be used instead of the butter.

FRIED EGG PLANT.

Pare and slice the egg plant, put in salted water over night; in the morning, drain, and dip each slice in a batter, or dip in bread crumbs, then in beaten egg, and again in crumbs; fry in drippings, or butter, until tender and brown. Serve hot.

LIMA BEANS.

Soak beans over night; cook 1 hr. in water enough to cover them; cook until nearly all the water is boiled away. Just before lifting, season with salt, pepper, a little cream and butter; let come to the boil again.

BOILED BEANS.

1 qt. beans, 1½ hp. tbsp. butter.
Juice ½ lemon, salt, pepper.

Cook the beans in boiling water until tender. When done, drain, shake over fire until dry, but still hot; add the butter, seasoning and lemon juice. Serve at once.

CARROTS COOKED IN STOCK.

Scrub, scrape and slice 5 or 6 large carrots; cook in boiling, salted water until half done; drain, add 2 c. stock, and 1 tsp. sugar; cook until the carrot has absorbed nearly all the stock; stir in 1½ hp. tbsp. butter, and if not salty enough, add a little. When the butter is well mixed with the carrot, serve.

SMOTHERED GREEN STRING BEANS.

Melt 1 large tbsp. of bacon or ham fat in a stew pan; add 1 tbsp. flour, and cook until brown. Thin with 1 pt. hot water; add ½ pk. beans, stringed and broken into small pieces; if not enough water to cover them add a little more. Simmer until tender. Season.

BATTERS.

APPLE FRITTERS.

4 apples, 2 tbsp. lemon juice,
2 tbsp. powdered sugar, ¼ tsp. cinnamon.

Pare your apples, core, and cut in slices, leaving the hole in the center. Spread on a plate and sprinkle with the other ingredients.

FRITTER BATTER.

1 c. flour, 2 eggs, ½ tsp. salt, ½ c. milk,
1 tsp. sugar, ½ level tbsp. butter, melted.

Mix the flour, salt and sugar together, separate the eggs, beat the yolks until creamy, add milk, and pour into the flour; melt butter and stir it in; beat well; fold in the whites, beaten stiff. Dip the slices of apples in the batter; cover well; fry in a bath of fat. Be careful not to break the slices of apple. Any kind of fruit may be used.

WAFFLES.

1 c. flour, ½ tsp. Rumford baking powder,
¼ tsp. salt, 2 eggs, generous ½ c. milk,
½ tbsp. butter, melted.

Sift flour, salt and baking powder, separate eggs, beat yolks until creamy; add milk, stir into flour, add butter melted, and lastly fold in the whites beaten stiff. Fry on a greased waffle-iron.

BUCKWHEAT CAKES.

3 tbsp. molasses, 3½ c. flour,
4 c. lukewarm water, 1 tbsp. salt,
¼ cake compressed yeast, dissolved in ¼ c. luke-

warm water. Mix the water, molasses, stir in the flour and salt, beat well, pour in the yeast. Let rise over night.

BUCKWHEAT CAKES—Made With Baking Powder.
1 tbsp. molasses, 1 tsp. salt,
1 qt. luke-warm water,
2 tsp. Rumford baking powder.
Generous 1½ pts. buckwheat.

Add molasses, salt and buckwheat to the water, beat well, stir in baking powder. Bake quickly.

FLANNEL CAKES.

2 c. flour, 2 tsp. Rumford baking powder,
½ tsp. salt, 2 c. milk,
2 eggs, 2 tsp. butter.

Sift flour, salt, and baking powder together. Separate the eggs, beat yolks, and pour in milk; stir into the flour, beat well. Put in butter melted; fold in whites. Dip out 1 tbsp. of the batter to form each cake. Fry on a greased griddle. When the cakes bubble they are ready to turn.

POP-OVERS.

1 c. flour, 1 c. milk, scant,
½ tsp. salt, 2 eggs.

Mix the dry ingredients together. Beat the eggs until full of bubbles; stir into the flour gradually; beat well. Fill gem pan two-thirds full, which has been greased; bake from 20 to 30 minutes. Serve hot, as a muffin for breakfast, or make a sauce and serve as a pudding.

CORN FRITTERS.

2 eggs, 1 tbsp. of cream,
1 c. bread crumbs, 1 can corn, or ½ doz. ears.
Salt and pepper.

Mix all together; fry in tbsp. butter; serve hot.

CORN CAKES.

2 eggs, 1 qt. milk.
Pinch salt, meal enough to make a thin batter.

Separate the eggs, beat the yolks until creamy; stir in meal and salt; beat well; add whites, beaten stiff. Bake very thin on a hot griddle, or add ½ tsp. baking powder and enough meal to make them thick, and bake in muffin pans in a hot oven.

TANGLED THREADS.

1 c. flour, 2 eggs.
½ tsp. salt, ½ c. milk.
2 tsp. sugar, 1 tbsp. butter.

Mix the dry ingredients together; separate the eggs, beat the yolks until creamy; add the milk to them and stir into the dry ingredients; melt the butter, and lastly fold in the whites beaten stiff. Fry in a bath of fat, run through a funnel or drop off a spoon in a thin stream; sprinkle with powdered sugar. Serve with a syrup.

BREAD FRITTERS.

Cut slices of bread thin, soak in milk one minute, cut a slice of bacon, and put between two slices of bread; dip in a batter and bake until brown. Serve hot, with an egg on top.

POTATO PAN-CAKES.

Sift together 2 c. flour, ½ tsp. salt, 1 tsp. Rumford baking powder, then add slowly 1½ c. milk, lukewarm, mix well, stir in carefully 1½ c. grated apples, fry in a frying pan, brown on both sides, or bake in the oven. When done, remove carefully from the pan; spread with butter and sprinkle with sugar, or maple syrup. Serve for breakfast, or with a sauce for lunch.

DROP FRITTERS.

Separate four eggs, beat the yolks until creamy, stir in slowly

1 c. milk, ½ tsp. salt, and 2 tbsp. butter melted, add 2 c. flour, lastly fold in the whites, beaten stiff, drop by the spoonful into a bath of smoking hot fat. Brown both on one side, then on the other; drain, sprinkle with pulverized sugar; serve hot with maple syrup.

EGG FRITTERS.

Scald 1 qt. milk in a double boiler; remove from the fire and stir into the milk 1 pt. soft bread crumbs, and 1 hp. tbsp. butter; cover and soak three-quarters to one hour. By that time the bread will have absorbed nearly all the milk. Then beat to a paste; separate 4 eggs, beat the yolks until creamy, and add to the bread, also ½ tsp. salt, 2 tbsp. sugar, ½ tsp. nutmeg, and ½ tsp. cinnamon; mix well; add 1 tsp. Rumford baking powder and 1 c. currants; then add the whites, beaten stiff. Drop into a bath of fat, and cook for about three min. Drain, roll in pulverized sugar. Serve with a sauce as a pudding, or for breakfast with maple syrup.

RICE WAFFLES.

Separate 2 eggs, beat the yolks until creamy; add to them 1 c. cold cooked rice, 2 c. milk, 1 tsp. salt, 2 tbsp. melted butter, 2 c. flour, (into which 2 tsp. Rumford baking powder has been sifted.) Lastly, fold in the whites beaten stiff. Fry in waffle-irons.

PEACH FRITTERS.

Put 1 c. water, ½ c. butter and 1 c. flour (into which has been put a large pinch soda), into a sauce-pan. Do not put the flour in until the butter is melted; then stir while adding the flour. Cook about two or three min., stirring rapidly all the time; set away to cool. When cold, add 4 eggs, one at a time; beat well. After the last egg has been put in, beat about five min. Pare and stone peaches, or use can peaches; cover each half with the batter, drop in a bath of fat and fry about three or four min.;

drain, sprinkle with pulverized sugar and cinnamon. Serve hot for breakfast. If you use canned peaches, they may be served as a dessert, making a sauce from the juice.

CEREALS.

STEAMED RICE.

½ c. rice, 3 c. milk,
1 tsp. salt.

Look over the rice carefully, wash well, and put in the top of a double boiler, with the milk and salt. Cook 2 hrs., after cooking 1 hr. stir with a fork, and if dry, add a little more milk; then cook until done. Serve with soft custard.

BAKED RICE.

1 c. rice, 2 qts. milk,
1 tsp. salt.

Put rice, salt and milk in a baking pan, put in a moderate oven in the morning; cook all day without stirring. In case it gets too dry, add more milk. Serve hot, with sugar and cream.

CORN-MEAL MUSH.

2 pts. boiling water, 1 c. corn-meal,
1 tsp. salt.

Mix the corn-meal and salt, pour into the boiling water, stir well. Boil 40 minutes to 1 hour. Cook in a double boiler 3 hours. When ready to fry, pack in a pan. Cut in ½ in. slices, and brown both sides in hot fat.

ROLLED OATS.

3 c. boiling water,
1 tsp. salt,
1 c. rolled oats.

Look the oats over carefully, and put with the salt and water, in the top part of a double boiler. Steam for 1 hr., or longer. Serve with baked or steamed fruits, sugar and cream.

RICE APPLES.

Cook the quantity for steamed rice. Core and pare six large apples. See that the rice is done. Cold rice may be used. Spread enough rice on a cloth that will cover an apple; put in apple; fill the center with sugar, and tie the cloth so that the apple will be covered with rice when done. Steam, boil, or bake until apples are done; remove cloth; serve with sugar and cream, or use as a breakfast dish, with maple syrup.

WHOLE WHEAT GEMS.

1 c. cream, (sweet or sour), 1 c. sugar,
½ tsp. salt, 2 c. whole-wheat flour.

Mix all together; knead until stiff enough to roll thin; cut and bake on un-greased tins in a hot oven.

ENTIRE WHEAT GEMS.

2 c. entire wheat, 1 tbsp. sugar,
½ tsp. salt, 1 c. milk,
2 eggs, scant c. water,

Separate eggs, add milk to the yolks (well beaten), mix wheat, sugar and salt, pour in milk, and then add the water; lastly, fold in the whites, beaten stiff. Bake in hissing hot gem pans 30 min.

STEWED FRUITS.

PRUNES.

Wash and soak 1 lb. prunes in cold water two hours. Cook in the same water until tender; five minutes before done add 4 tbsp. sugar and 1 tbsp. lemon juice. Set away to cool.

CRANBERRIES.

1 pt. cranberries, 1 c. cold water, 1 c. sugar.

Look over and wash the cranberries, put in an agate sauce pan the berries and water. Cook closely covered for 10 min.; strain, then add the sugar; cook five min. longer.

STEAMED RHUBARB.

1 pt. rhubarb, 1 c. sugar.

Wash and peel the rhubarb, cut into small pieces, put in the top part of a double boiler; add the sugar, and steam until tender. Do not stir until done.

PEACHES.

Wash and soak the peaches in cold water, drain, and add to 1 lb. peaches, ½ c. boiling water. Cook until tender. A few min. before done, add ¾ c. sugar.

APPLE SAUCE.

Wash, pare and core the apples, (tart,) put in a sauce pan, ½ c. water; when boiling add six apples. Cook, mash through a strainer, sweeten to taste; 1 c. sugar; serve.

STEWED RHUBARB.

Wash and scrape the rhubarb, cut in inch pieces, put in a sauce pan, with just enough water to keep it from burning; cook until soft. To 1 c. rhubarb add ½ c. sugar. Cook five min. longer.

BAKED PEARS.

Cook eight pears until half done, in a syrup made from 1 pt. water, and ½ c. sugar. Put pears in a baking dish, sprinkle with sugar, about 3 tbsp.; bake until soft. Cook syrup until 1 c. and melt in it 4 tbsp. grated chocolate. Add 4 tbsp. whipped cream. Flavor with vanilla, pour over pears. Serve hot or cold. It is a nice breakfast dish.

RHUBARB JELLY.

Cook 1 qt rhubarb (do not peel), with ½ c. water, 1 c. sugar, until soft, or steam without water, which is much better. Soak 3 oz. gelatine in a little cold water, ½ hr. Dissolve by adding the boiling rhubarb, pour into moulds. When hard serve with whipped cream. Be sure the rhubarb is sweet enough.

CANDIES.

PEANUT CANDY.

Melt 1 c. granulated sugar in a sauce-pan, stirring all the time (do not add any water). When melted stir in 1 c. chopped peanuts, or any kind of nuts. Mix well, spread on a tin which has not been greased; press into shape with a knife. Do it quickly as it hardens immediately.

CHOCOLATE CARAMELS.

1 c. sugar, 1 c. molasses,
½ c. milk, ½ c. chocolate,
1 tbsp. butter, tsp. vanilla.

Mix all together, excepting the vanilla; cook slowly until it hardens in cold water; add vanilla and pour out on buttered tins; cut in squares. To make nut caramels, add chopped nuts, after removing from the fire.

PEPPERMINTS.

Moisten 1 c. sugar with water. Cook until it ropes, without stirring, add peppermint and beat until it thickens, drop on wax paper. Orange mints may be made by using the juice instead of water, also lemon mints.

BUTTER CARAMELS.

2 c. sugar, ½ c. butter,
½ c. vinegar, 3 tbsp. molasses.

Mix all together, and boil until it will crisp in water, and be very careful not to cook too long, or it will sugar.

STUFFED DATES.

Cut open each date, remove the stone and in its place put an almond. Press the edges together and roll in granulated sugar.

BUTTER SCOTCH.

1 c. sugar, 1 c. molasses,
½ tsp. vanilla, ½ c. butter.

Boil all together until brittle, when dropped in cold water, add vanilla and pour into greased pans.

CHOCOLATE FUDGE.

1 c. grated chocolate,
3 lbs. brown sugar,
1 c. milk.

Mix. Cook hard ten min., remove to the back of the stove, and cook 10 min. longer, and beat hard. Pour into greased pans.

COCOANUT BALLS.

Grate 1 large nut and put in a cool place. Take 1 lb of granulated sugar, and add to it ½ c. water; place on the stove and boil until about ready to sugar, remove it at once, and add cocoanut. When nearly cool make into balls.

CHOCOLATE ALMONDS.

Blanch and dry the almonds. Melt sweetened chocolate or sweet chocolate and in this stir the almonds; when well covered take out with a fork, and drop on buttered paper. Melt the chocolate over steam.

SALTED ALMONDS.

Shell and blanch the almonds, dry well, and spread thinly in a shallow pan; add a little butter and brown. Be careful not to burn. When done remove from the oven, and while hot sprinkle with a little salt; stir well. Set away to cool.

CREAM CANDIES.

2 lbs. confectioner's sugar,
White 1 egg,
Equal amount of water,
Flavoring.

Mix the egg and water together, stir in the sugar a little at a time; beat well. You can make any kind of candy, using the cream in making chocolate drops. Shape the cream and when dry dip in bakers' chocolate, melted; lift with a fork and drop on wax paper, cool. Almonds, English walnuts, dates or, in fact, any kind may be made. Roll all but the chocolate drops in granulated sugar.

ICE CREAM CANDY.

2 c. sugar, 1 c. water,
1 tbsp. vinegar, tsp. vanilla.

Boil the sugar, water and vinegar until crisp when dropped in cold water; do not stir; remove from the fire, pour on buttered dish or plate; when cold enough pull until white; add vanilla while pulling. Do not grease your hands.

PRALINE.

1½ lbs. brown sugar,
½ c. milk, 1lb English walnuts.

Mix sugar and milk; cook hard 5 to 10 min., stirring constantly; add nuts chopped fine, cook 10 min. longer, beating all the time; remove from the fire and continue beating until creamy. Pour on buttered pans, and cut in squares before it gets too hard.

MAPLE CREAMS.

2 c. maple sugar, 1 c. water,
Small piece of butter.

Cook the sugar and water, without stirring; before done add the butter. When it begins to harden when dropped in water, remove from the fire and stir rapidly until it becomes a waxen substance; then form into balls; put between two walnuts, and put on a greased plate to cool.

CRYSTALIZED POP-CORN.

Put 1 tbsp. butter in a granite sauce-pan, 3 tbsp. water, and 1 c. granulated sugar; boil until crisp when dropped in cold water, then stir in 3 qts. of nicely popped corn; mix well, so that every grain will be covered. Be careful that the fire is not too hot, or the corn may burn after it is put into the sugar. Form into balls before too cold. You can flavor the syrup with 1 tsp. of any kind of extract. Nuts may be crystalized the same way.

BUTTERED POP-CORN.

Have 1 pt. corn popped; put into a large bowl, and sprinkle freely with salt; melt ½ c. butter and while hot pour over the popcorn; mix well, and keep where it is warm, so that the butter will not become hard. It is very nice to eat as soon as prepared.

TWISTED COLORED CANDY.

Cook 3 lbs. of white sugar and 1 pt. of water until brittle when dropped in cold water; pour out on three buttered steak platters, (remember, do not stir the syrup while cooking). When cold enough to handle, add three drops of any fruit coloring you want; also the flavoring desired, and pull until well mixed, and very nearly cold. Twist or braid the three colors together; then roll very thin and cut in small pieces, or as large as you desire.

CREAM CHOCOLATES.

Mix 2 c. brown sugar, ¾ c. milk, 2 tbsp. butter, 3 hp. tbsp. grated chocolate, in a sauce-pan; put on the stove and cook until (when a little of the mixture is dropped in ice water) it will harden; stir often; then add ½ c. (extra) sugar, and 1 tbsp. vanilla; beat a few min., pour into well-buttered pans, about ¾ in. Set away to harden. When nearly cold, mark off in squares. These creams can be made in warm weather as well as cold.

CHOCOLATE CREAMS.

Put into a sauce-pan 1 c. water and 2 c. granulated sugar; stir until the sugar is dissolved; put on the stove, cook slowly, without stirring. When it begins to boil, cook about ten min., or until it hardens enough, when dropped, to roll into a little ball between the fingers. Take from the fire, and stir in 5 hp. tbsp. chocolate; let stand until cool, then stir with a spoon until thick. Work with the hand until creamy and smooth. Flavor with ½ c. vanilla.

This may be made in balls, dropped into colored icings, or, put a small piece of cream between English walnuts; also place a little between two vanilla caramels; the cream for the chocolate caramels is made the same way, only omit the chocolate and use not so much vanilla. Chocolate drops may be made of this cream, by shaping them, then dip in melted chocolate.

FIG CANDY.

Cook 1 pt. water and 1 lb. sugar over a slow fire until crisp when dropped in cold water. When done, add ½ tbsp. vinegar, and the same of butter, and pour over the figs, which have been cut in small pieces, and put in a greased pan.

NUT GLACE.

Cook 1 c. sugar and ½ c. water, without stirring, until brittle Just before removing from the fire, add 1 tsp. butter and ¼ tsp. vanilla. Have ready any or all kinds of nuts; either pour the boiling syrup over the nuts in a buttered pan, or dip each nut on a fork into the syrup; then lay on a buttered pan or greased paper. Great care must be exercised in making nut glaces, as there is danger of it going to sugar. In case it should, put on enough water to dissolve the sugar; then cook again, as in the beginning.

CHOCOLATE BUTTER-SCOTCH.

1 c. molasses, 1 c. sugar.
½ c. butter, 1 c. chocolate.
1 tsp. vanilla.

Cook all the ingredients, excepting the vanilla, until crisp when dropped in cold water; remove from the fire, stir in the vanilla, pour into buttered pans; cut in squares before too cold.

SUGAR KISSES.

Beat the whites of 3 eggs, stiff; add ¾ c. of pulverized sugar, sifting it in lightly. Drop by spoonfuls on paper placed on the bottom of pans. Put in the oven with the door open for half an hour. Then brown slightly. Nut kisses may be made by adding a few finely chopped nuts. These kisses are also used as meringues.

MARSHMALLOWS.

Dissolve ½ lb. of white gum arabic in 1 pt. of water; strain, and add ½ lb. pulverized sugar; place over the fire, stirring constantly until the ingredients are dissolved, and of the consistency of honey. Add gradually the whites of 4 eggs, beaten stiff; stir the mixture until it becomes somewhat thin, and does not adhere to the fingers. Flavor to taste with vanilla, and pour into a tin slightly dusted with powdered starch, and when cool divide into small squares.

EGGS.

FOAMY OMELET.

2 eggs, 2 tbsp. milk,
½ tsp. salt, pinch pepper.

Separate the eggs; beat the yolks until creamy; add salt and pepper, beat again; then milk, and lastly fold in the whites beaten stiff. Melt 1 tsp. butter in a pan. When it bubbles pour in the omelet. Let it cook slowly for 5 min. on the top of the stove then; put on the grate of the oven for 2 or 3 min. to dry.

BAKED EGGS.

Separate the eggs (being careful to keep the yolks whole), allowing the yolks to remain in the half-shell. Beat the whites stiff and spread on slices of softened and buttered toast; drop the yolks in the centre, season with a little salt and bake a golden brown.

FLOUR OMELET.

1 tsp. butter, 2 eggs,
2 tsp. flour, ½ c. milk,
¼ tsp. salt, pinch pepper.

Melt the butter, add flour, salt and pepper, and pour in the milk. Separate the eggs; beat the yolks until creamy; add to the sauce. When cold, fold in the whites beaten stiff. Cook the sauce as the Foamy Omelet.

MEAT OMELET.

Make foamy omelet and add to it any kind of cold chopped meat. Oysters or stewed tomatoes, chopped parsley may be added if desired.

EGG VERMICELLI.

Moisten and butter toast. Make a sauce of 1 tbsp. butter, 1 tbsp. flour, 1 c. hot milk, salt and pepper. Cook 2 eggs hard. Chop the whites in small pieces, and add to the sauce; pour over the toast and rub the yolks, through a strainer, over the sauce.

STUFFED EGGS, NO. 1.

3 hard cooked eggs, 1 tbsp. chopped meat.
Salt and pepper, pinch mustard,
Spk. cayenne, a little cream.

Cut the eggs in halves, length wise, and mash the yolks, and mix with them the other ingredients, fill the whites and serve on a small steak platter; garnish with parsley.

PICKLED EGGS.

½ doz. hard cooked eggs.
1 pt. vinegar (not too strong).
Bay leaf, pinch cayenne.
½ tsp. salt.

Use cold vinegar; mix the other ingredients with it; pack eggs in glass jar; pour the mixture over eggs and securely fasten; keep for months in a cool place.

STUFFED EGGS, NO. 2

4 hard cooked eggs.
1 c. crab meat, juice 1 lemon.
1 tbsp. chopped parsley.
1 tbsp. butter, ½ tsp. salt.

Cut the eggs, lengthwise, mash the yolks and to them add the other ingredients; mix well, refill the whites; lay on a steak platter and garnish with water cress. This is for lunch; it may be served as a breakfast dish, by pouring a cream sauce over the eggs.

CREAMED EGGS FOR BREAKFAST.

1 tbsp. butter, 1 tbsp. flour,
1 c. milk, ½ tsp. salt,
1 tbsp. parsley, pinch pepper, 4 eggs.

Melt the butter, add flour, salt, parsley and pepper, thin with the milk, pour into a buttered baking dish, not very large, so that the sauce may be ½ in. thick; break four eggs into the sauce, be careful you do not break the yolks; bake in a hot oven until the eggs are firm. This may be used for lunch, but add 2 hp. tbsp. grated cheese to the sauce.

EGGS WITH MUSHROOMS.

Cut ½ can mushrooms into small pieces, slice 1 large onion; cook in tbsp. butter; boil 4 eggs hard, cut the whites into small pieces, put mushrooms, onion, and whites into a sauce-pan, pour on 1 c. stock; simmer 20 min. Season. Cut the yolks in thin slices, and add just before removing from the fire. Pour over toast. Serve hot.

CURRIED EGGS.

Mix 2 tsp. curry to a paste with stock 1½ c.; let it simmer until reduced to 1 c.; blend 1 tbsp. butter and 1 tbsp. flour, and add to the stock. Cook 4 eggs hard, cut into slices, add; let come to a boil, and serve very hot.

BAKED EGGS, No. 2.

Butter a baking dish, drop in as many eggs as are desired, without breaking the yolk; season with salt and pepper; put in a moderate oven, and cook until the white is firm.

BAKED EGGS No. 3.

Take large tomatoes, cut out the core, making a cup; break 1 egg into the center, sprinkle with salt and pepper; put in a baking pan and cook until the white of the egg is firm. Serve or a piece of moistened and buttered toast. Make a brown sauce and pour over the toast.

CHOCOLATE OMELET.

Separate 4 eggs, beat the yolks until creamy; add to them ¼ c. cream, ½ tsp. salt, and a pinch of pepper; beat well; **then add 1 tbsp. chocolate**, melted, and lastly fold in the whites, beaten stiff. Melt 1 tbsp. butter in a frying-pan, and when the butter is melted and hissing, pour in the omelet. Set on the back part of the stove until omelet is firm in the bottom; then set on the grate of a hot oven until golden brown. Serve on a round plate, garnished with parsley.

EGGS WITH CREAMED BEEF.

Put 1 lb. chip beef in cold water, and when it comes to a boil cook 15 min.; drain off water. Blend 1 tbsp. butter and 1 tbsp. flour; pour on the beef, 1 c. milk and ¼ tsp. salt. When it comes to a boil stir in the flour and butter. Cook 5 min. Toast 4 large slices of toast, soften by dipping in hot milk, lay on a hot platter, pour the beef over the toast, (if not salty enough, add a little more). Poach 4 eggs and lay on each piece of toast. Serve hot, or it may be served in this way: Just before lifting the beef, poach the eggs and put in a dish. Pour the creamed beef over them. Still another way: Drop the eggs into the beef before lifting, and let cook until the eggs are done. Serve on toast. Great care must be taken in cooking them this way, so that the yolk of the egg will not be broken.

CHEESE.

MACARONI AND CHEESE.

2 c. broken macaroni, ¼ lb. cheese (grated).
2½ c. milk, 1 tbsp. butter,
½ tsp. salt, spk. cayenne,
1 egg (if desired).

Cook the macaroni in hot water 20 min., stirring constantly; pour off water and add milk, cook 10 min. longer; remove from the fire; add ¾ of the cheese, butter, salt and pepper, and egg well beaten; pour into a buttered baking dish; sprinkle on the rest of the cheese; bake in a hot oven until brown.

WELSH RAREBIT.

8 tbsp. grated cheese, 2 eggs,
¼ c. milk, cream or beer,
¾ tsp. mustard, ½ tsp. salt,
1 tsp. butter, pinch cayenne,
6 small slices of toast.

Mix all dry ingredients together, add eggs well beaten, rinse out bowl in which the eggs were beaten with milk, stir into the mixture also butter; cook in double boiler until cheese is melted; pour over toast.

CREAMED TOAST.

1 c. hot milk, 1 tbsp butter,
1 tbsp flour, ½ tsp. salt.
Pinch pepper.

Toast 2 slices of bread, sprinkle on each slice enough cheese to cover; sprinkle with white pepper, set in the oven until cheese is melted, then pour over the sauce, made by melting the butter, add flour, seasoning, and lastly the hot milk. Cook 5 min.

CHEESE FONDU.

1 c. rolled crackers, 1 c. milk,
⅔ c. grated cheese, 2 eggs (separated).
Seasoning.

Mix crackers, cheese and milk, add yolks beaten light, salt and pepper; fold in whites beaten stiff. Bake in a hot oven 20 to 25 min.

CHEESE SOUFFLE.

1 tbsp. butter, 1 c. cheese.
1 hp. tbsp. flour, 2 eggs.
½ c. milk, ½ tsp. salt.
Spk. cayenne, pinch soda.

Melt the butter, add flour and seasoning, stir in slowly the hot milk; cook 5 min.; add cheese; yolks beaten creamy and soda, beat well; stand aside to cool. When cold fold in whites beaten stiff, pour into a buttered baking dish and bake in a slow oven until brown. Serve at once.

CRACKERS AND CHEESE.

Take soda crackers or in fact any crackers, spread with butter, grated cheese and pepper, toast in a hot oven until the cheese is melted and the crackers browned.

SCALLOPED CHEESE.

Cook ½ c. rice in 1½ c. stock for 1 hr., grate 1 c. cheese; when the rice is done remove from the fire and add cheese, yolks of 2 eggs beaten creamy, salt and pepper, a little chopped parsley; line a baking dish with bread crumbs softened with butter, fold in whites and pour into the dish; make a crust of bread crumbs, and bake in oven.

CHEESE FINGERS.

Roll pastery into thin sheets. Over half of it spread grated cheese, sprinkle with white pepper; fold double and cut in strips 1 in. wide and 3 in. long. Bake in a hot oven 12 min.

CHEESE PUFFS. No. 1.

2 tbsp. butter, 1 c. boiling water,
5 tbsp. flour, ½ tsp. salt,
5 tbsp. grated cheese, 2 eggs,
Pinch cayenne.

Melt the butter in the boiling water; mix flour, salt and pepper and cheese together; add to the boiling water; cook 5 min.; stirring all the time, remove the from the fire, beat until cold; add eggs, one at a time (do not beat until added to the mixture), beat 15 min. Bake on a buttered pan in a moderate oven 20 to 30 min.; do not put them close together. Serve with either white or brown sauce.

CHEESE PUFFS. NO. 2.

Beat the whites of 2 eggs stiff; add to them 1 hp. tbsp. of grated cheese, salt and pepper; drop by the tsp. into a bath of fat. Cook 3 min.; drain, garnish with parsley; serve at once.

CHEESE BALLS.

Stir into the yolks of 3 eggs ½ lb. grated cheese, bread crumbs to make a stiff dough, add a little salt and cayenne. Make into balls with a thin wrapper of puff paste, and fry in a bath of fat.

CHEESE BISCUITS.

Soak ½ doz. stale biscuits in 1 c. milk, 10 min.; then add 1 c. grated cheese, butter, stir the cheese, biscuits, pinch salt and cayenne pepper together; pour into a buttered pudding dish. Cut 1 tbsp. butter in small pieces and put on top. Bake in a hot oven until brown, 20 to 30 min.

BREAD WITH CHEESE SAUCE.

Make a sauce by melting 1 tbsp. butter; add 1 tbsp. flour, ½ tsp. salt, pinch cayenne, and a pinch mustard; thin with 1 c. hot milk; let boil 5 min.; then stir 3 hp. tbsp. cheese. Cook until the cheese is melted; dip 3 slices of toast or stale bread in hot milk, put on a hot platter, and pour the cheese sauce over them. Take two hard cooked eggs and chop, add to the cheese sauce before pouring over the toast or bread, is an addition. This is a nice breakfast dish. Serve hot.

CHEESE EGGS.

Cook 3 eggs hard, remove the yolks without breaking, take the white of 1 raw egg and beat until very stiff, add enough grated cheese to make it stick together; season with salt and cayenne pepper, roll the hard cooked eggs in this mixture, covering them well; fry in a bath of smoking hot fat until a golden brown. Make a white sauce; cut the whites in small pieces; put into the sauce. Place the cheese eggs on a hot platter, and pour the sauce around, not over, them. Garnish with parsley.

COTTAGE CHEESE.

Heat sour milk slowly until a whey rises to the top; pour it off; put the curd in a bag, and let drip six hours, without squeezing it. Put into a bowl and chop fine, with a wooden spoon. Season to taste with salt, and work to a soft paste with sweet cream. Serve in balls, or add more cream and serve in a dish, sprinkled with white pepper. Keep on ice an hour or two before serving.

CHEESE CAKES.

1 large c. grated cheese, 1 c. sugar, the grated rind of 1 lemon, and juice of ½ lemon, ½ c. soft bread crumbs, 4 eggs, 1 tbsp. butter, melted, ½ c. cream, ¼ tsp. salt. Mix the crumbs with the cheese, stir well, beat the eggs with the sugar, and add to the cheese and crumbs, melt butter, stir in, also cream. Lastly, add the lemon juice and rind. Mix all well together and put into well-buttered muffin-pans. Bake 15 or 20 min., in a quick oven. They will puff up, but do not let them get too brown. These cakes may be made as one, baking in a pan. When done, cut in squares. These cakes are nice served with a brown or white sauce, with roasts, or serve at lunch, with just the sauce.

CUSTARDS.

BAKED CUSTARD.

1 pt. milk, 4 eggs.
½ c. sugar, ¼ tsp. salt.
Nutmeg or vanilla.

Beat the eggs, add the salt and sugar; pour on the milk very slowly, add vanilla (if nutmeg, grate on top); bake in cups or in a dish; set in a pan of hot water in a moderate oven; test as directed for custards.

COCOANUT BREAD CUSTARD.

2 eggs, 1 pt. milk.
3 tbsp. sugar, pinch salt.
1 c. cocoanut or 1 small can of condensed cocoanut,
3 slices of bread (buttered).
1 tsp. vanilla.

Beat eggs, salt and sugar, pour in the milk and vanilla, add cocoanut, cut bread in squares, pour custard into a baking dish, put bread on top, pushing down with spoon. Bake about 30 min.

TAPIOCA CREAM.

2 tbsp. tapioca, 5 c. milk.
3 eggs, ½ c. sugar,
Pinch salt, 1 tsp. vanilla.

Soak tapioca in 1 c. of the milk over night, or take 4 tbsp. pearl tapioca, and put in the top part of a double boiler with ½ c. hot water, and cook until the water is absorbed, add the rest of the milk, and cook until tender; separate the eggs and to the yolks add the sugar and salt; pour in the milk, return to the boiler and cook until like soft custard; beat whites stiff and stir into the tapioca; flavor, set away to cool, or pour tapioca into cups; beat whites stiff, add 2 tbsp. of powdered sugar put on top and bake in the oven until a light brown.

SPANISH CREAM.

Soak one box of gelatine in 1 c. milk 2 hrs.; scald 1 qt. milk in double boiler; pour over gelatine, beat the yolks of eight eggs and add to the gelatine (always pour the hot into the cold), sweeten with 1½ c. sugar; return to the boiler and cook until thick as for custard; beat whites until stiff and pour in the custard; mix well, flavor with 1 tsp. vanilla, and let cool in a mould.

WINE CREAM.

½ oz. gelatine soaked in 1½ c. white wine until soft, add the juice and grated rind of 1 lemon and 1½ c. sugar; put on stove until gelatine is dissolved; strain and when cool, but not congealed, add 3 c. cream, stirring gently, that it may not separate.

APPLE FLOAT.

1 qt. stewed apples.

Whites 3 eggs, 4 hp. tbsp. sugar.

Mash apples, sweeten and stir in whites beaten stiff; beat twenty min.; serve as soon as done, with sugar and whipped cream. Strawberry, peach or in fact any fruit may be used.

FLOAT.

1 qt. milk, yolks 3 eggs.

1½ tbsp. corn-starch.

Heat milk, blend the cornstarch with a little cold milk, and stir into the hot milk; beat yolk and pour over them the milk, return to the boiler and cook until thick; sweeten to taste. Beat the whites; pour boiling water over them in a bowl; then lift off and put on custard. You may omit the starch and use 4 eggs.

SNOW CUSTARD.

½ box gelatine, 3 eggs (yolks),
2 c. sugar 3 tbsp. sugar,
1 c. cold water, pinch salt,
1½ c. boiling water, 2 c. milk,
½ c. lemon juice,
Whites 5 eggs, ½ tsp. vanilla.

Soak the gelatine in cold water 1 hr. or until soft, dissolve by adding the boiling water, stir in sugar and lemon juice, strain, set away to cool; when it begins to stiffen add the whites beaten stiff, and beat until stiff enough to drop; pour into a mould. Make a custard of the yolks, add the 3 tbsp. sugar, salt and milk; cook in a double boiler; when done flavor; serve with the snow.

VELVET CREAM.

1 qt. milk, 1 c. sugar,
¼ box rose gelatine, 1 tsp. cornstarch,
Flavoring.

Blend the cornstarch with part of the milk, soak the gelatine in it; scald the remainder and when the gelatine is soft dissolve in the hot milk, sweeten and cook in double boiler 15 min., stirring all the time; flavor with vanilla, and set aside to cool; serve with cream or whipped cream.

BAVARIAN CREAM.

½ box gelatine, 1 pt. cream,
½ c. cold water, ¼ c. sugar,
1 tsp. vanilla, 1 tbsp. wine, (if desired),
or ¼ c. orange juice.

Soak the gelatine in the cold water. Whip the cream until all is whipped but half cup, put with 1½ c. milk and scald; pour over the gelatine; beat the yolks of the eggs and add salt, sugar and dissolved gelatine; cook in top part of boiler 3 min., stir, strain into a bowl set in ice water. When cool add flavoring and wine or orange juice; stir until it begins to thicken, then fold in quickly the whipped cream; when nearly stiff pour into a mould.

GELATINE WHIP.

Line a mould or dish with lady fingers, make a whip of
2 c. milk, 4 eggs.
4 tbsp. sugar, ½ box gelatine.
½ c. cold water, 2 c. cream.
½ c. boiling water, 1 tbsp. vanilla.
1½ c. pulverized sugar.

Make a custard of the yolks of the eggs, the 4 tbsp. granulated sugar and the milk. Set away to cool; when the gelatine has soaked in the cold water 1 hr. dissolve by adding the boiling water. Whip the cream until stiff, also the whites of eggs, add to them the powdered sugar, stir into the custard (when cold), the whipped cream, the whites and then the gelatine, flavor; pour into the mould or dish; set away to harden.

CHARLOTTE RUSSE.

½ box gelatine, ½ c. cold water.
1 qt. cream, 2 doz. lady fingers.
1-6 c. powdered sugar. 1 tsp. vanilla.
½ c. boiling water, 1 tbsp wine.

Soak the gelatine in the cold water until soft; line a dish or mould with the cakes, leaving the crust side out. Whip the cream; keep the pan in ice water; sift the sugar over the cream, and add vanilla and wine if used; pour the boiling water over the gelatine and when dissolved add to the cream, then stir slowly, keeping the pan in the water; be careful that it does not get lumpy; if it should, remove from pan and stir it in a warm place; when stiff enough to drop pour into mould.

CARAMEL CUSTARD.

½ c. sugar, 6 eggs.
2 tbsp. water, 1 qt. milk.
½ tsp. salt, 1 tsp. vanilla.

Put the sugar in an omelet pan, and stir until it melts and is light brown; add the water, and stir into the warm milk. Beat the eggs slightly, ad'd the salt and vanilla, and part of the milk, strain into the remainder of the milk, and pour into a greased mould. Set the mould in a pan of warm water, and bake 30 to 40 min., or until firm. Test as for custards. Serve with caramel sauce.

BRANDY CUSTARD.

Strain the juice if 1 lemon over 4 tbsp. granulated sugar, and add 2 tbsp. brandy; pour this mixture into 1 qt. cream; whip until quite thick. Serve in glasses.

WHITE FOAM.

Line a pretty dish with macaroons. Whip 1 pt. cream until thick; soak 1 tbsp gelatine in ¼ c. cold water ½ hr.; dissolve in ½ c. hot milk, strain into the cream, stirring constantly, sweeten with 2 tbsp. powdered sugar, flavor with 1 tsp. vanilla; set in a pan of ice water, and as soon as it begins to thicken put lightly in the dish, set on ice 2 hrs. Serve with whipped cream.

LEMON CREAM.

Blanch and chop ½ c. almonds, and put in a bowl with 1 pt. cream; whip, sweeten to taste; add 1 c. sherry wine, juice 2 lemons. Serve in glasses.

LEMON CUSTARD.

Let the juice of 3 lemons, 5 hp. tbsp. sugar, 2 c. boiling water come to a boil; strain; separate 8 eggs; beat the yolks until creamy; pour the boiling syrup over the eggs, stirring constantly. Put in top part of double boiler, cook until it begins to thicken; fold in whites beaten stiff. Let stand until perfectly cold.

PUDDINGS.

ALBANY PUDDING.

Grease a bowl, thick with butter, put seeded raisins around it, then line with bread crumbs; make a custard like "Cup Custard" and pour in the centre, bake until the custard is done; eat with a liquid sauce.

BANANA TAPIOCA PUDDING.

Soak 1 c. pearl tapioca in cold water 1 hr. Put in top part of double boiler, with 1 c. boiling water and ½ c. sugar; cook ¾ hr. Cut bananas in thin slices, sprinkle with powdered sugar and a little lemon juice; put a layer of bananas in the bottom of the dish, then pour on the tapioca; make as many layers as you desire, but always have the bananas on the bottom and top; serve.

DUTCH PUDDING.

1 pt. flour, 2 tsp. Rumford baking powder.
½ tsp. salt, 2 eggs, 1 c. milk,
3 tbsp. butter, 1 c. sugar,
½ c. hot water, ½ tsp. nutmeg,
1 qt. cut apples.

Reserve 2 tbsp. of the sugar. Put the apples, sugar and water into a baking dish, add nutmeg and lemon juice; bake until the apples are partly soft; mix flour, the 2 tbsp. sugar, baking powder and salt together; beat the eggs well and add them to the milk; stir into the flour until smooth; melt butter and add it; spread this mixture over the apples; return to the oven and bake for 30 min. Serve with lemon sauce.

STEAMED BERRY PUDDING.

1 c. sugar, 2 eggs, 2 c. flour,
1½ tsp. Rumford baking powder, 1 c. milk,
2 c. berries.

Beat the eggs; add to them sugar, milk, berries and flour, in which baking powder had been sifted; steam 2 hrs. in a buttered pudding dish, covered by a cloth.

BOSTON PUDDING.

1 c. sugar, 2-3 c. butter,
½ lb. suet chopped, 2 c. milk,
1 c. flour, 1 c. bread crumbs,
2 tsp. Rumford baking powder, 2 tbsp. molasses,
1 c. seeded raisins, pinch salt.

Mix according to order, and boil in a bag 4 hrs.; serve with hard sauce.

BROWN BETTY.

Grease a pudding dish; sprinkle in the bottom a layer of soft bread crumbs; then nearly fill the dish with alternate layers of crumbs and sliced peaches; sprinkle with sugar, nutmeg and small pieces of butter; if can peaches are used pour the liquor over them, if not, and the peaches are very dry use a little water; have a crust of bread crumbs; bake 1 hr. or until the fruit is soft.

PEACH PUDDING.

3 tbsp. rice, 1 pt. milk,
2 tbsp. sugar, 2 eggs,
A little lemon peel,
Stick of cinnamon,
1 pt. peaches.

Cook the rice and milk with the sugar, lemon peel (cut in small pieces) and cinnamon for 1 hr.; remove the cinnamon and let the rest cool, when cool add the yolks, well beaten; pour into a buttered baking dish; put the peaches on top (if the fresh fruit; cook in a syrup made from ½ c. sugar and ½ c. water until tender. Make meringue of the whites and 2 tbsp. pulverized sugar; spread on the pudding and brown in a cool oven.

BREAD PUDDING.

3 eggs (separate), 3 pt. milk.
1 c. sugar, 1 tsp. vanilla.

Cut the bread into squares, buttering before doing so; beat the yolks and to them add sugar, milk and vanilla; put bread into a baking dish; pour the milk over it and bake in a moderate oven 45 min. When done make a meringue of the whites and 2 tbsp. powdered sugar, spread on top and bake till a golden brown.

COTTAGE PUDDING.

2 eggs (separate), 1 c. sugar,
1 c. milk, 2 tbsp. melted butter,
½ tsp. salt, 2 tsp. Rumford baking powder,
2 c. flour.

Cream the butter, sugar and yolks of eggs, add salt and milk, stir in flour, in which baking powder was sifted, fold in the whites; bake or steam.

ENGLISH PLUM PUDDING.

2½ lbs. raisins, 2 lbs. sugar,
2 lbs. currants, 2 lbs. bread crumbs,
2 lbs. suet, 6 oz. candied lemon peel, 1 grated nutmeg, 1 oz. cinnamon, ½ oz. almonds, ½ pt. brandy, rind 2 lemons, 16 eggs.

Butter and flour a pudding cloth. Mix all the ingredients together; put into a cloth tie; be sure the water is boiling before you put in the pudding. Boil 8 or 9 hrs., or steam 24 hrs. This pudding will keep for weeks.

COCOANUT PUDDING.

2 qts. milk, 6 eggs.
1 cocoanut, grated; sweeten to taste.
Small piece of butter.

Mix all together and bake until firm; stir once before it thickens.

CHOCOLATE PUDDING.

½ lb. chocolate.
1 qt. milk, 3 eggs, ½ tbsp. cornstarch.

Dissolve the chocolate in the hot milk; sweeten to taste and flavor with vanilla. Beat the yolks and cornstarch together. When the milk is at the boiling point stir in the eggs; cook until it thickens; pour in a dish (the one to be brought to the table). Beat the whites, spread on top with chopped almonds and coarse sugar sprinkled on top; brown slightly.

FIG PUDDING

1 c. sugar, 1 egg.
½ c. flour, ½ tsp. soda.
1 c. milk, 1 c. figs.

Mix the flour, sugar and soda together; blend the milk with the egg and add to the flour; stir in the figs, cut in small pieces; steam; serve with foamy sauce..

CHRISTMAS PLUM PUDDING.

1 lb. suet, 1 lb. currants.
1 lb. raisins, 8 eggs.
½ nutmeg, (grated), 2 oz. candied peel.
1 tsp. ground cinnamon, ½ tsp. ground cloves.
½ lb. soft bread crumbs, 2 c. flour.
1 c. milk.

Chop the suet and mix with the dry ingredients, stir well; add eggs well beaten and milk, tie in a floured bag; boil for 5 or 6 hrs. or longer.

FIG PUDDING, No. 2.

Chop fine 1 lb. figs; add 3 c. soft bread crumbs, 1 c. sugar, ½ c. melted butter, 4 eggs, beaten light, and 1 c. sweet milk. Mix well, steam for 2 hrs. in a buttered pudding dish. Serve with Wine Sauce.

HASTY PUDDING.

Let 1 qt. milk come to a boil; add a large pinch of salt, then stir in ½ c. flour and 1 egg. Cook for five min., stirring all the time. Serve with sugar and cream.

STRAWBERRY PUDDING.

Make a custard of 2 eggs, 1 pt. milk, 2 tbsp. sugar and 1 tsp. of vanilla. When perfectly cold, pour over 1 basket of strawberries, which have been picked, washed and sprinkled with pulverized sugar. Set on ice and let stand ½ hr.

PINEAPPLE GLACE.

Soak 1 c. pearl tapioca in enough cold water to cover it, over night; in the morning, put on in double boiler with 1 c. sugar, and cook until clear and tender. Pare 1 good-sized pineapple, and remove all specks and chop fine; pour over the boiling tapioca, and mix well; pour into a mould, and when perfectly cold, serve with whipped cream.

FRUIT PUDDING.

Line a glass dish with stale pieces of cake or bread, and fill with any or all kinds of fruit. Soak 1 tbsp. gelatine in ½ c. cold water; dissolve by pouring over it 2 c. boiling milk; beat 1 egg until light, sweeten with 1 c. sugar, add milk and gelatine, return to the double boiler, and cook until thick like soft custard. When cold pour over the fruit and cake. Serve with plain or whipped cream.

RAISIN PUDDING.

Take 1 egg and beat until light; add 1 c. sugar, and 2 tbsp. butter, melted; ½ c. stoned raisins, 2 c. flour, and 1 tsp. Rumford baking powder. Steam 1 hr. Serve with Hard Sauce.

CHOCOLATE PUDDING.

2 c. flour, 1 c. milk,
2 eggs, 2 tbsp. butter, melted,
½ c. sugar, pinch salt,
2 tsp. Rumford baking powder,
4 hp. tbsp. chocolate, melted.

Mix all the dry ingredients together. Separate the eggs, and beat the yolks until creamy; add milk and pour into the dry ingredients; stir in butter; mix well, add melted chocolate, and lastly fold in the whites, beaten stiff. Pour into a well-greased pudding dish, and steam from 1½ to 2 hrs. Serve with creamy sauce.

FRUIT PUDDING.

Soak 1 c. stale bread in 2 c. milk. Put in a double boiler; add 1 tbsp. butter, 1 c. sugar, ½ tsp. of salt, and ½ tsp. spice. Remove from the fire. When cool, add 3 eggs, well beaten. Add 2 c. of fruit, peaches, strawberries or apricots. When using canned fruit, drain it from the syrup, and use the juice in making a sauce. Vary the sugar accordingly. Put in a greased pudding dish, and steam 2 hrs., or bake 1½ hrs. Serve with a sauce.

CARROT PUDDING.

2 c. flour, 1 c. sugar,
½ lb. chopped suet,
½ lb. currants, ½ tsp. salt,
½ lb. grated carrots.

Mix in the order given, and steam in a buttered mould 3 hrs. Serve with wine sauce.

PUDDING SAUCES.

WHIPPED CREAM SAUCE.

1 c. cream, whites 2 eggs.
½ c. powdered sugar, 1 tsp. vanilla.

Whip cream vanilla and sugar without skimming, add whites beaten stiff. Beat all together. Serve with any kind of cold pudding or dessert.

HARD SAUCE.

1 c. butter, 1 c. fine sugar, nutmeg.

Cream the sugar and butter together, add nutmeg. Keep in a cool place. Serve with a hot pudding.

CREAM SAUCE.

c. milk, 1 c. sugar, 3 tbsp. cornstarch.

Boil a few min., then add 1 tbsp. of butter and 2 tbsp. brandy.

FOAMY SAUCE.

1 c. sugar, 2 eggs, 3 tbsp. cold water.

Set over a tea-kettle of boiling water, stir all the time until well cooked. Then add a tbsp. butter. Flavor to taste. Serve with fig pudding.

LEMON SAUCE, No. 1.

1 c. sugar, ½ c. water.
Rind and juice of two lemons.
Yolks of 3 eggs, 1 tbsp. butter.

Boil the water, sugar, and lemon rind, for 20 min., beat the eggs, and pour into the syrup; add juice and butter. Serve hot.

LEMON SAUCE, No. 2.

1 c. sugar, 3 tsp. cornstarch,
1 tbsp. butter, 2 c. boiling water,
Juice and rind of 1 lemon.

Mix the sugar and cornstarch together, pour on the boiling water, stirring all the time; boil 10 min. When ready to serve, add rind, juice and butter.

NUTMEG SAUCE.

2 c. boiling water, ¼ tsp. salt,
1 c. sugar, 1 tbsp. cornstarch,
2 tsp. nutmeg, 2 tbsp. butter.

Blend the cornstarch and sugar together, add the boiling water, salt and nutmeg. Simmer 20 min. Add butter and strain.

CUSTARD SAUCE.

2 eggs, ⅛ tsp. salt,
2 tbsp. sugar, 2 c. milk, ½ tsp. vanilla.

Prepare and cook just like soft custard.

WINE SAUCE.

½ c. butter, 1 c. sugar,
5 tbsp. wine.

Cream the butter and sugar, until light, heat the wine and add a tbsp. at a time; beat well, set in a pan of boiling water for 1 min. Serve.

WINE SAUCE.

Put 1 c. water into a sauce-pan, and when it comes to a boil add 1 c. sugar, 2 tbsp. butter and 2 eggs, (which have been mixed together); let cook 3 min. When removed from the fire, add ½ c. of wine.

BRANDY SAUCE, No. 1.

Blend 1 tbsp. sugar and 1 hp. tbsp. of butter together; then pour on ½ c. boiling water; cook 10 min.; add 1 scant c. brandy. Serve boiling hot.

BRANDY SAUCE, No. 2.

After beating 1 c. butter to a cream, gradually beat in 2 c. pulverized sugar; then slowly add ½ c. of brandy. Set the bowl in which the butter and sugar are in into a pan of boiling water, and stir until the sauce is creamy. Sprinkle a little nutmeg on top, if desired. Serve in a hot sauce dish or pitcher.

FRUIT JUICE SAUCE.

Make a syrup of 1 c. sugar, 2 c. boiling water, and 1 c. sour fruit juice. Cook five min. When ready to serve, add 1 hp. tbsp. butter. Serve with sweet puddings.

CARAMEL SAUCE.

Melt 1 c. sugar, stir in ½ c. boiling water; cook 5 min.; add 1 tbsp. butter. Serve hot.

BROWN SAUCE.

Rub to a cream 2 c. light brown sugar, and ½ c. butter; add ½ c. weak wine, a little at a time. Just before serving, set in a pan of boiling water until hot.

APPLE SAUCE.

Cook 1 c. apples until soft; mash through a fine sieve; add ½ c. sugar; let stand until thoroughly cold. Scald 1 c. milk; pour over 1 egg, beaten light, put back in double boiler, and let it cook until like soft custard. Remove from the fire and when cold add the apples. This is a nice sauce for a very sweet pudding.

CHEAP SAUCE.

Thicken 1 c. boiling water with 1 tsp. flour moistened in a little cold water; cook 5 min. When ready to serve, stir in 1 tbsp. sugar, 1 tbsp. butter, and 1 tsp. of any kind of flavoring, or a pinch of nutmeg or cinnamon.

CINNAMON SAUCE.

Put 1 c. sugar and 1 c. boiling water into a sauce-pan, with a stick of cinnamon, about 5 in., and simmer for ¾ to 1 hr. Remove cinnamon, and add 1 tbsp. butter. Strain and serve.

ORANGE SAUCE.

Boil 1 c. water and ½ c. sugar together for 10 min. When cold, add the rind of 2 and the juice of 4 oranges. Let stand on ice until ready for use. Then strain. This sauce is to be served with a cold pudding.

SALADS.

CHICKEN SALAD.

1 qt. chicken, 1 pt. celery,
2 tbsp. chicken stock, 1 tbsp. vinegar,
Small bowl salad dressing.
Salt and pepper.

Cook the chicken, and when cold cut the meat into small pieces, or dice; mix the stock and vinegar together and pour over the chicken. When ready to use, either strain this off or let it remain on; season and add "Salad Dressing."

VEGETABLE SALAD.

Cut into dice all kinds of cold cooked vegetables, season, and serve with salad dressing or mayonnaise.

TOMATO SALAD No. 1.

Skin 6 tomatoes, cut out the heart, scoop out a little of the inside and mix with it a little onion juice, chopped parsley, and 1 hp. tbsp. cold cooked meat, chopped very fine. Either serve with a little vinegar mixed with it, or salad dressing. Refill the tomato cups. Serve on lettuce leaves, with a little mayonnaise on top.

TOMATO SALAD No. 2.

1 pt. tomato juice, 1 box gelatine,
½ c. cold water, ½ c. boiling water, salt.

Soak the gelatine in the cold water 1 hr., add boiling water, when dissolved, season, pour into small round moulds, and set away to harden. Serve on lettuce leaves, with mayonnaise.

TOMATO SALAD No. 3.

Skin 6 tomatoes, remove heart, cut out a little of the tomato, making a cup; put the tomatoes on ice, and with what you scooped out, add a little chopped celery, cucumber, parsley, and onion, if desired. Refill the tomato cups. Serve on lettuce leaves, with a "Yellow Dressing."

BEEF SALAD.

2 c. meat, 2 c. cabbage.
1 tbsp. celery seed or ½ c. chopped celery.
2 tbsp. sugar, salt and pepper; Dressing.

Any or all kinds of cold cooked meat can be used. Cut the meat in small pieces, and chop th cabbage fine; add celery, sugar and seasoning; mix well and pour on any good salad dressing.

POTATO SALAD.

1 pt. cold boiled potatoes, 1 tbsp. onion juice,
1 tbsp. chopped parsley, 2 hard cooked eggs.
Seasoning, "Salad Dressing."

Cut the potatoes into dice, and to the dressing add the onion juice and parsley. Cut the eggs in small pieces and add also a little chopped celery, if desired. Serve on lettuce leaves, garnished with hard-cooked eggs.

CABBAGE SALAD, or COLD SLAW.

Cut fine, firm, crisp cabbage, let it stand in cold water a few min., drain well, pour over Hot Salad Dressing, and set away to cool. When ready to serve, arrange neatly in a pretty dish.

FISH SALAD.

1 c. fish, 3 hard cooked eggs,
2 cold boiled potatoes,

Use any kind of cooked fish. Cut the whites of eggs in small pieces, also the fish; mash the yolks and thin with a little cream, or vinegar (if liked sour), mix all together, season, serve on lettuce with "Cold Salad Dressing."

CELERY SALAD.

1 large bunch celery, 2 hard cooked eggs.
½ c. cabbage, chopped fine.
1 tsp. sugar, ¼ tsp. mustard.
Salt and pepper, vinegar.

Mix all together, and moisten with the vinegar.

VEAL SALAD.

1 lb lean veal, 2 hard cooked eggs.
1 c. celery, seasoning.

Cook the veal, and cut in dice, also the celery, chop the whites of the eggs and add with the seasoning; make "Foamy Salad Dressing;" when ready to use, mash the yolks and thin with a little of the dressing.

LOBSTER SALAD, No. 1.

1 lb. veal, 3 hard cooked eggs.
1 green pepper, salt, 2 tbsp. vinegar.
Small head lettuce, 1 bunch celery.
1 can lobster.

Cook the veal. When cold, chop all together; mix with any salad dressing. Serve garnished with hard cooked eggs.

LOBSTER SALAD, No. 2.

1 can lobster, 2 heads lettuce.
½ c. soft bread crumbs.
4 hard cooked eggs.
1 small bunch celery.
1 bowl yellow salad dressing.

Cut the celery in small pieces, reserve the better leaves for serving; chop the other leaves and add to the celery also the rest of the ingredients. Chop the eggs, not fine, mix well and serve on lettuce leaves, with crackers.

SHRIMP SALAD.

Boil 1 pt. of shrimps until tender, about 20 min.; when cold add to 1 qt. cabbage and 1 bunch celery chopped fine; serve with any kind of dressing.

SWEET POTATO SALAD.

Boil 3 large sweet potatoes. Peel and cut into ½ inch squares. Cut into small pieces 2 stalks of celery. Season, and pour over a salad dressing. Serve on lettuce, garnished with pickles.

OYSTER SALAD.

Cook 1 qt. oysters in their own liquor a few min. Skim and strain; season the oysters with 2 tbsp. lemon juice, 1 tbsp. salad oil, ½ tbsp. salt, pinch cayenne pepper; set on ice for an hr or two. Chop 1 pt. celery and mix with the oysters. When ready to serve, arrange in a pretty dish, and pour over a mayonnaise dressing, garnished with celery tops.

TOMATO AND CUCUMBER SALAD.

Place a bed of crisp lettuce in a salad bowl; then lay in a layer of thin sliced tomatoes; then sliced cucumbers. Continue so doing, until the dish is full, having tomatoes for the top layer. Pour over the whole Boiled Salad Dressing.

SWEETBREAD SALAD.

Cook a pair of sweetbreads in boiling water, with ½ tsp. salt. Cook until tender. Drain, and when cool cut into dice. Measure. Pare and cut a cucumber in small pieces. Have the same amount of each. Season with salt and cayenne pepper. Arrange on lettuce leaves, on a steak platter, and pour over a good salad dressing. Garnish with pickles.

EGG SALAD.

1 doz. hard cooked eggs.
3 tbsp. butter, 2 tbsp. vinegar,
2 tsp. salt, pinch cayenne.

Remove the shells, and cut each egg in half. Take out the yolks, rub through a fine sieve, add the butter, melted, vinegar, salt and pepper; mix thoroughly and fill the halved whites. Serve on lettuce leaves; put a little mayonnaise on each half.

CHOPPED LETTUCE SALAD.

Take 1 head of crisp lettuce; cut into small pieces. Cut 3 hard cooked eggs into dice, add to the lettuce, season with salt and pepper. (if celery may be had, chop ½ c. and add). 1 small onion, grated. Mix with 1 c. cooked salad dressing. Serve in a salad dish.

GREEN-BEAN SALAD.

Season 1 qt. of cold, boiled, green string beans, cut into pieces, with French dressing. Serve on lettuce, garnished with olives. Yellow beans may be used in place of the green, or even lima beans may be used.

CUCUMBER SALAD.

Peel and slice 1 large, or 2 small, cucumbers as thin as possible; sprinkle with ½ tsp. salt and pepper mixed. 1 tbsp. vinegar, not too strong, and 3 tbsp. salad oil.

SLICED CUCUMBERS.

Peel and slice a cucumber in thin slices (do not put in salt water, as salt toughens them), serve on chipped ice, with salt, pepper and sour cream, or sliced onions and vinegar.

SALAD DRESSING.

BOILED SALAD DRESSING.

1 c. vinegar, 2 eggs,
2 tsp. flour, ¼ tsp. mustard,
Pinch cayenne, 3 tbsp. sugar,
1 tsp. salt, 2 tbsp. salad oil, (if desired).

Beat the eggs, heat the vinegar, and pour over the eggs, stirring all the time. Mix all the other ingredients together and add. Cook until it begins to thicken, stirring constantly. Remove and beat well. You can use butter instead of the oil.

COLD SALAD DRESSING.

Rub the yolks of 4 eggs fine, season with salt, pepper and a little mustard; thin with 5 tbsp. of rich, sour cream, and 1 tbsp. vinegar.

HOT SALAD DRESSING.

2 eggs, 1 tsp. salt,
Pinch pepper, 1 tbsp. sugar,
3 tbsp. melted butter, 4 tbsp. vinegar,
2 tbsp. water.

Heat the water and vinegar, add the butter, seasoning and sugar; when boiling pour over the eggs. Serve on cold slaw.

SALAD DRESSING.

2 eggs, 1 tbsp. butter,
6 tbsp. vinegar, ½ tsp. salt,
Pinch pepper.

Heat the vinegar, pour over the beaten eggs, return to the

stove, as soon as it begins to thicken, remove, stir in the butter and seasoning, beat until smooth; if too thick, thin with a little cream.

MAYONNAISE.

Yolks of 2 eggs, 1 tbsp. powdered sugar.
¼ tsp. mustard, ½ tsp. salt.
Pinch cayenne, 1 c. oil.
Juice 1 lemon, 4 tbsp. vinegar.

Beat the yolks, salt, mustard, pepper and sugar, until thick, then add the oil a little at a time, beat a few min., every time you add the oil. When all the oil is in, beat for 5 min. Add lemon juice and vinegar; beat well; set away in a cool place until ready for use.

FOAMY SALAD DRESSING.

3 eggs, 1 tbsp. sugar.
½ c. milk, ¼ c. vinegar.
1 hp. tbsp. butter, 1 tsp. salt.
¼ tsp. mustard, pinch cayenne.

Heat the milk, separate the eggs, beat the yolks until creamy, add mustard, salt, pepper and sugar, pour in the hot milk, also hot vinegar very slowly, return to the double boiler, add butter, and stir. Cook until like soft custard, beat the whites until stiff, remove top part of double boiler, fold in the whites.

YELLOW DRESSING.

1 tbsp. flour, ½ tbsp. sugar.
¼ tsp. mustard salt.
Cayenne, 4 tbsp. vinegar.
1 scant c. boiling water.
2 eggs, 1 tbsp. butter.

Mix the dry ingredients together; blend with the vinegar; pour in slowly the boiling water, stirring all the time. Cook 5 min. Add butter; remove from the fire and add the egg, well beaten. If too thick, thin with sweet or sour cream. It will keep weeks.

CAKES.

---o---

In making a cake, be sure and use a baking powder with acid phosphate. "Rumford" is the only one I find that comes up to the standard.

DEVIL'S FOOD No. 1.

Part First—
    1 c. brown sugar, ½ c. butter.
    2½ c. flour, ½ c. sweet milk.
    2 eggs, 1 scant tsp. soda.
Part Second—
    1 c. grated chocolate, ½ c. sweet milk.
    2-3 c. brown sugar, 1 egg, 1 tsp. vanilla.

Part First—Cream butter and sugar together, separate eggs, beat yolks and add to the butter and sugar, stir in flour and milk, alternately; lastly fold in whites, beaten stiff. Before adding soda, make Part Second—Melt the chocolate in a sauce pan, add egg (do not separate), brown sugar, milk and vanilla; beat well; dissolve soda in a little water, pour into Part First; then add Part Second. Mix well, but do not beat. Bake either in layers or solid.

DEVIL'S FOOD No. 2.

Part First—
    1 c. brown sugar, ½ c. butter,
    2 c. flour, ½ c. sweet milk.
    Yolks of 3 eggs, 1 scant tsp. soda, sifted in the flour
Part Second—
    Melt 1 c. grated chocolate, ½ c. sweet milk, 1 c. brown sugar; When cool, stir into part first.

SPONGE COCOANUT CAKE.

1 doz. eggs, 1½ lb. granulated sugar
¾ lb. flour, 1 hp. tsp. Rumford baking powder.
1 tsp. vanilla.

Separate the eggs and to the beaten yolks add the sugar, vanilla and beat well, stir in the flour, in which the baking powder has been sifted, fold in the whites, beaten stiff, bake in layers, in a moderate oven about 30 min. Use two grated cocoanuts, and boiled icing.

FRUIT CAKE.

1 lb. butter, 1 lb. pulverized sugar,
1 lb. flour (browned) 1 doz. eggs,
2 lbs. raisins, 2 lbs. currants,
½ lb. citron, 1 lb. figs,
1 c. walnuts, 1 c. almonds,
1 tbsp. ground cloves,
1 tbsp. ground allspice,
2 tbsp. ground cinnamon,
1 nutmeg grated
Wine glass brandy.

Cream the butter and sugar, add the yolks, well beaten, then the flour and fold in the whites beaten stiff, chop the nuts and mix with the fruit which has been cut in small pieces, flour all and add to the mixture, stir well, add the brandy, bake in a moderate oven three hrs.; when done will weigh eight pounds.

ANGEL CAKE.

Whites 9 eggs, 1 c. flour,
1½ c. granulated sugar, 1 tsp. vanilla,
1 tsp. cream tartar.

Beat the whites until stiff, sift in the sugar carefully (which has been sifted several times), then the flour (having gone through the same process as the sugar), with the cream of tartar in it stir, do not beat, flavor; bake in an ungreased pan, in a moderate oven 45 min.

POUND CAKE.

Cream, 1 lb. butter, add 1 lb. pulverized sugar and the yolks of 12 eggs, beaten light, stir in flour and beat well, fold in whites, beaten stiff; bake as a solid cake in a moderate oven one hr. This cake depends upon the beating.

SUNSHINE CAKE.

1 c. butter, ¾ c. milk,
2 c. sugar, 1 tsp. vanilla,
Yolks 9 eggs, 2 c. flour.
2 tsp. Rumford baking powder.

Cream the butter and sugar add the yolks, well beaten, and vanilla, beat well, add the milk and flour, alternate (keeping out about 2 tbsp.), beat well, sift in the rest of the flour, with the baking powder mixed in it. Bake, either as a solid or layer cake.

PERFECTION CAKE.

3 c. pulverized sugar (sifted four times),
1 c. butter, 1 c. sweet milk,
3 c. flour, 2 tsp. cream of tartar.
Whites 12 eggs, ½ tsp. soda,
1 c. cornstarch, vanilla.

Cream butter and sugar, dissolve the cornstarch in ¾ of the milk, and add to the sugar and butter (dissolve the soda in the rest of the milk) add flour, beat well, then pour in the soda, also the cream of tartar, sifted in a little of the flour, flavor, lastly, fold in the beaten whites; bake as a solid cake.

CHOCOLATE CAKE.

½ c. butter, 1 c. sugar, 4 eggs, 2 c. flour.
2 tsp. baking powder (Rumford).
1 tsp. vanilla 2 tbsp. boiling water,
4 hp. tbsp. grated chocolate.

Cream the butter and sugar, separate the eggs and add the

yolks; melt the chocolate in the boiling water and add, beat well, flavor, add the milk and flour, also baking powder, lastly the beaten whites; bake in layer 30 min.; ice with a white icing.

FRENCH CREAM CAKE.

1 c. butter, 1½ c. flour,
1 c. sugar, 2 tsp. Rumford baking powder,
Yolks 3 eggs,
1 tsp. vanilla.

Bake in layers. Mix according to rule. The filling for the cake.

½ pt. hot milk,
½ c. sugar, ¼ c. butter,
1 egg, 1 tbsp. cornstarch,
½ tbsp. vanilla.

Blend the cornstarch with a little cold milk; and pour into the hot milk in top part of double boiler, sweeten, stir this into the beaten egg; cook until the consistency of very thick custard; just before removing from the fire add the butter; set away to cool, flavor, spread between the cake.

ALMOND CAKE.

4 eggs, ¼ tsp. soda
1 c. sugar, pinch salt,
1 c. flour, flavoring,
½ tsp. cream of tartar.

Beat the whites and yolks separately then together add the sugar lightly, carefully stir in the flour and cream of tartar, lastly the soda, dissolved in cold water; bake in layers in a moderate oven.

FILLING.

Soak ½ box gelatine in enough cold water to cover it, for 1 hr. then dissolve in ½ c. sherry wine, which has been heated. Beat the whites of five eggs very stiff, add 1 c. cream and sweeten to taste, also flavor with vanilla, add the dissolved gelatine to the cream, when cool, but before it thickens, stir in 1 lb. of chopped almonds (blanched), keeping a few for the top.

BLACKBERRY CAKE.

1 c. butter, 3 c. flour.
2 c. sugar, 2 tsp. Rumford baking powder.
Yolks 5 eggs, 1 c. blackberries.
1 c. milk, whites 5 eggs.

Mix in order. Solid cake.

A RELIABLE CAKE.

½ c. butter, 1 tsp. Rumford baking powder.
1 c. granulated sugar, 1½ c. flour.
2 eggs, ½ tsp. vanilla.
½ c. milk.

Mix in order given. A marble cake may be made by adding chocolate to part of the mixture; also a nut cake by adding nuts.

MARSHMALLOW CAKE.

½ c. butter, 3 c. flour.
2 c. sugar, 1½ tsp. Rumford baking powder.
½ c. milk, whites 8 eggs.

Mix in order. Bake in layers and between the layers put the following filling:

2 oz. fine gum Arabic.
8 tbsp. warm water.
8 hp. tbsp powdered sugar.
Whites four eggs, 1 tsp. vanilla.

Soak the Arabic for 1 hr. in the water, then put in top part of double boiler; keep the lower part half full of boiling water, stir constantly until the Arabic is dissolved, strain through cheese cloth, add sugar, stir until dissolved; beat the whites until stiff, and pour the mixture over them, flavor. When cool it should be light and thick; do not use on cake until perfectly cold (cake), as the warm cake will melt the gum.

FRENCH LOAF CAKE.

1 c. butter, ½ lb. raisins,
1½ c. sugar, ¼ lb. currants,
Yolks 3 eggs, 2½ c. flour,
1 c. wine, 3 tsp. Rumford baking powder,
2 tsp. ground cloves, whites 3 eggs,
2 tsp. ground cinnamon.

Mix in order given; bake in a loaf pan.

CARAMEL CAKE.

Cake,—

2 c. sugar, 1 c. milk,
3 c. flour, 1 small c. butter,
Whites 4 eggs, 2 hp. tsp. Rumford baking powder,

Caramel,—

2 c. dark brown sugar or maple,
1 butter, 2 c. sweet cream.

Mix caramel all together and boil not so long as for candy. Mix the cake according to rule, use the caramel for the filling between the layers.

SPICE CAKE.

½ c. butter, 1½ c. sugar,
4 eggs, ½ c. milk,
2 c. flour, 1 tsp. cream of tartar,
½ tsp. cinnamon, ½ tsp. soda,
1 tsp. grated nutmeg, ½ tsp. cloves.

Mix according to the general rule.

RED, WHITE AND BLUE CAKE.

¼ c. butter, 1 c. sugar,
1 tsp. Rumford baking powder,
½ c. milk, 1½ c. flour,
Whites 3 eggs, 1 tsp. vanilla.

Cream the butter and sugar; add flour and milk, also flavoring, baking powder, and lastly fold in the whites beaten stiff. Divide in three bowls; in one put ⅓ tsp. blue fruit coloring; in another put the same amount of red; keep the third white. Bake in layers.

WHITE CAKE.

1 c. butter, 2 c. sugar.
Whites 8 eggs, 1 c. milk.
1 tsp. soda, 2 c. flour.
1 c. cornstarch, ¼ tsp. salt.
3 tsp. almond essence.
2 tsp. cream of tartar.

Mix according to rule.

VANILLA CAKE.

½ c. butter, 1½ c. sugar.
3 eggs, 2 c. flour, ½ c. milk.
2 tsp. Rumford baking powder.
1 tsp. vanilla.

Mix according to rule; bake in layers, and put cream filling between, and ice with plain icing.

GOLD AND SILVER CAKE.

"Gold"—

½ c. butter, 1 c. sugar, yolks 6 eggs.
1¾ c. flour, 2 tsp. Rumford baking powder.
1 tsp. vanilla.

Cream the butter and sugar, add yolks, beat well, then the extract and flour, beat hard; lastly add the baking powder; make into one layer; bake 20 to 30 min.

"Silver"—

½ c. butter, 1 c. sugar.
Whites 6 eggs, 1¾ c. flour.
1 hp. tsp. Rumford baking powder.
1 tsp almond.

Make the same as for gold, only fold in the whites, beaten

stiff, the last thing. This will make two layers. Put the gold in the center.

ORANGE CAKE.

1 c. sugar, ½ c. butter,
2 c. flour, ½ c. milk,
Yolks 4 eggs, whites 3 eggs,
2 tsp. Rumford baking powder.

Cream the butter and sugar; separate the eggs; beat yolks until creamy, and add to the sugar and butter; beat well; then stir in milk and flour alternately (into which the baking powder has been sifted), and lastly fold in the whites, beaten stiff, and 1 tsp. orange juice. Bake in four layers. For the filling, grate the rind of 2 oranges, and mix with the juice, and 1 c. pulverized sugar, put between the layers. Ice.

SPONGE CUSTARD CAKE.

4 eggs, 1 c. sugar,
1 c. flour, 1 tsp. cream of tartar,
¼ tsp. soda, pinch salt,
1 tsp. vanilla.

Beat the whites and yolks separately, then together. Add sugar, lightly stir in the flour, and lastly the soda, dissolved in a little cold water. Bake in a square cake pan in a very moderate oven. When cold, cut in squares, tear open with a fork, and put between a cream made from 1 c. milk, scalded, 1 c. sugar, ½ c. flour, 2 eggs, and ¼ tsp vanilla. Beat the eggs, mix the flour and sugar thoroughly, add to the beaten eggs, pour on the milk, and cook in a double boiler about 10 min., stirring while it thickens. When cold, flavor and put between the cake.

JELLY ROLL.

1 c. sugar, 1 c. flour,
3 eggs, 1 tsp. Rumford baking powder.

Mix all together; beat well; spread on a long, narrow baking tin; bake quickly in a hot oven; turn out on a cloth; spread with currant jelly and roll up.

WINE CAKE.

½ c. butter, 1½ c. sugar,
3 eggs, 2 c. flour,
1 tsp. Rumford baking powder.
½ c. wine.

Cream the butter and sugar, separate the eggs, add yolks to the butter and sugar; beat well, then add wine, and flour (into which the baking powder has been sifted), alternately, lastly fold in the whites beaten stiff. Bake as a solid cake, or in layers, with wine jelly between, and ice with boiled icing, flavored with wine.

GINGER POUND CAKE.

1 c. butter, 4 c. flour, 1 c. sugar, 1 c. milk.
2 c. molasses, 3 eggs, 1 tsp. cinnamon,
1 tsp. ginger, 1 tsp. cloves, 1 tsp. allspice.
1 tsp. soda (dissolved in a little boiling water).

Bake 1½ hrs. in moderate oven.

ALMOND CUSTARD CAKE.

1 lb. of pulverized sugar,
½ lb. of flour, 8 eggs,
1 tsp. of flavor.

Beat the yolks until light; then add the sugar, after sifting twice; then alternate the flour and beaten whites of eggs; then flavor. Bake in layer cake pans, spread the custard between layers, and ice the top.

Custard,—

Soak ¾ box of gelatine in as much cold water as will cover it, for 1 hr. Then dissolve it in ½ c. sherry wine, by heating it a little. Beat the whites of 5 eggs to a stiff froth; mix with the eggs a small cup of cream, and stir in enough sugar to sweeten it, and 1 tsp. vanilla. Stir the wine into this mixture. When it is cool, but before it becomes stiff, stir in 1 lb. of almonds, blanched and chopped fine, reserving some whole to ornament the top.

MOUNTAIN CAKE.

The whites of 10 eggs, 1 lb. of sugar.
1 lb. of flour, ½ lb. of butter, (light weight),
1 c. of milk, 2 tsp. Rumford baking powder.
Flavor to taste.

Bake in four cake pans, spread each leaf with currant jelly and icing; after laying them one to top of the other, ice the whole in a mass.

GOLD CAKE.

The same as the above, substituting the yolks of 10 eggs instead of the whites; flavor with lemon; spread each leaf with custard, then ice the whole.

Custard.—
1 tbs. cornstarch, the yolks of 3 eggs.
1 pt. milk, sugar to taste; flavor with vanilla.

Icing.—
The whites of 3 eggs, 1 lb. of pulverized sugar,
1 tsp. vanilla.

RELIABLE SPICE CAKE.

1 c. butter, 1 c. milk, 2 c. sugar.
4 c. flour, 5 eggs, 1 tsp. cloves.
2 tsp. soda, 1 tbsp. cinnamon.
½ lb. citron, 1 lb. currants,
1 lb. raisins, 1 nutmeg.

Beat the butter until light, then add the sugar, eggs, milk and flour; then the spices, and then fruit, well floured. Lastly, the soda, wet with boiling water. Bake two hours in a moderate oven.

ICINGS.

BOILED ICING.

1 c. granulated sugar,
1-3 c. boiling water, white 1 egg,
½ tsp. vanilla.

Cook the sugar and water together, without stirring, until it ropes; beat the whites stiff, pour on the syrup slowly, beating well; when it thickens, flavor and spread on the cake, in case it sugars add 2 tbsp. cold water.

FRENCH ICING.

Dissolve ½ tsp. gum Arabic in enough rose water to cover it (1 tsp.), beat the whites of 3 eggs stiff, and stir in enough sugar to make it very thick, add to it the rose water; spread with a knife wet in cold water.

CHOCOLATE ICING.

1 c. granulated sugar,
1-3 c. boiling water,
1 tsp. vanilla,
2 hp. tbsp. grated chocolate.

Boil the same as for boiled icing; while beating add the chocolate, melted over steam.

ALMOND ICING.

1 c. almonds,
1 c. powdered sugar,
Whites 2 eggs,
Little rose water.

Blanch the almonds dry and pound, making a paste, using

the rose water to soften them; beat the whites stiff, stir in the sugar and nuts. Be sure you have it smooth before putting on the cake.

CREAM FILLING FOR DEVIL'S FOOD.

1 c. cream, ½ c. sugar,
1 tbsp. butter, tsp. vanilla.

Cook altogether excepting the vanilla, for 10 min., stirring all the time, remove, beat until thick and creamy.

CARAMEL ICING.

½ c. sugar, ¼ c. boiling water,
½ tbsp. butter.

Melt the sugar with 1 tbsp. boiling water, when melted add the ¼ c. boiling water and stir in the butter, remove from the fire, beat until stiff enough to pour over the cake.

CREAM ICING.

1 c. cream,
1 level tbsp. powdered sugar,
½ tsp. vanilla.

Sweeten and flavor the cream and whip until thick, spread between and on the cake.

CHOCOLATE ICING, NO. 2.

6 tbsp. grated chocolate,
1½ c. sugar pulverized,
4 tbsp. cream, whites 4 eggs,
1 tsp. vanilla.

Put the chocolate, part of the sugar and cream in a sauce-pan and cook until thick and glossy; beat the whites until stiff, and add the rest of the sugar and flavoring; pour on the melted chocolate and beat until creamy.

YELLOW ICING.

To 1 c. powdered sugar, add 2 tbsp. water, 1 tsp. lemon juice and yolk 1 egg; beat well; pour over the cake.

BEVERAGES.

COFFEE, NO. 1.

4 tbsp coffee,
White 1 egg,
½ c. cold water,
1 qt. freshly boiling water.

Scald the coffee pot, put in the coffee, egg and cold water; mix well, pour on boiling water when it begins to boil; cook five min., stir down, set on the back part of stove and settle 2 min.

COFFEE, NO. 2.

4 tbsp. coffee,
White 1 egg,
1 qt cold water.

Mix all together and let stand over night; in the morning, as soon as it comes to a boil, stir down, settle.

TEA.

1 tsp. tea, 1 c. boiling water.

Use a granite tea-pot, put in tea and pour the water over it (freshly boiled), steep five min., do not boil.

PLAIN CHOCOLATE.

2 hp. tbsp. chocolate,
3 tbsp. sugar, 1 qt. milk,
2 tbsp. boiling water.

Heat the milk in double boiler, dissolve the sugar and chocolate in the boiling water and add to the milk; serve at once.

FRENCH CHOCOLATE.

4 sticks sweet chocolate,
3 tbsp. boiling water,
1 pt. hot milk,
4 tbsp. cold milk,
1 tsp. cornstarch.

Heat the milk, melt the chocolate in the boiling water; blend the cornstarch and cold milk, pour into the hot milk; cook 5 min., add chocolate and serve.

COCOA.

4 tsp. cocoa, 1 pt. milk,
1 c. boiling water, sweeten to taste.

Blend cocoa and boiling water, heat milk, sweeten, add to the milk; serve hot.

BREAD and DOUGHS.

BAKING POWDER BISCUITS.

2 c. flour, 1 tbsp. shortening,
2 tsp. Rumford baking powder,
½ tsp. salt, ¾ c. milk.

Sift the dry ingredients, work the shortening in with the tips of the fingers; add milk slowly; pat out gently, about ½ inch thick. Bake in a hot oven from 12 to 15 min.

DUMPLINGS.

Make the same as for biscuits, omitting the shortening; drop by tsp. on stews, sour kraut and potatoes. (one egg may be added). Steam, tightly covered, 10 min.

APPLE DUMPLINGS.

Use the receipe for biscuits, divide in five or six pieces, roll out large enough to cover an apple, press the edges together; bake 30 min., or steam 1 hr.

STRAWBERRY SHORT-CAKE.

2 c. flour, 2 eggs, ½ tsp. salt,
2 tsp. Rumford baking powder,
Scant c. milk, 1 tbsp. sugar. (desired).

Mix as for biscuits, stir in the milk and eggs, well beaten. Bake 20 to 30 min. 1 basket of berries is enough. Pick and wash the berries carefully; put in a dish, with enough sugar to make a syrup; stand on ice for about 1 hr. When the cake is done, split with a fork; spread a little butter on each piece.

When cool, add berries, put on top crust. Peaches, oranges, or, in fact, any fruit may be used.

POUNDED BISCUITS.

2 c. flour, ½ tbsp. sugar.
2 tsp. cream, ½ tbsp. butter.

Mix the flour, sugar and cream, work the butter with the tips of the fingers. Add enough water to make a stiff paste, scant ¾ c. Beat with a rolling-pin, 10 min. Roll very thin; cut, prick with a fork, and bake in a moderate oven about 10 min., until pale brown.

FRIED BISCUITS.

2 c. flour, 1½ tsp. Rumford baking powder.
1 tsp. butter, pinch salt.

Mix flour and powder together, work in butter. Make a dough thin enough to drop from a spoon, with sweet milk. Fry in a bath of fat until light brown.

MARROW-DUMPLINGS.

Mix 1 c. marrow, 1 egg, a little salt, and pinch nutmeg, enough flour to form a ball; roll in flour, and drop on stews. Cook about 10 min.

BREAKFAST BISCUITS.

1 c. sugar, 4 tbsp. butter.
1 egg, ½ c. milk, ½ tsp. soda.
Pinch salt, 2 c. flour.

Mix as for biscuits; roll ½ in. thick; bake from 10 to 15 min.

SWEET BISCUITS.

1 c. butter, 1 c. sugar.
2 c. flour, 1 egg.

Mix butter, flour and sugar together. Moisten with the egg

well beaten; roll about 1-3 in. thick; cut, and bake in a moderate oven about 15 min. A blanched almond may be put on each biscuit.

MUFFINS.

2½ c. flour, ½ tsp. salt,
2 eggs, 1 c. milk,
2 tsp. Rumford baking powder,
1 tbsp. butter.

Mix the dry ingredients; separate the eggs; add the milk to the well beaten yolks, stir into the flour, beat in the butter melted; lastly fold in the whites beaten stiff. Bake in muffin-pans from 25 to 30 min. in a moderate oven. Sweet muffins may be made by adding ½ c. sugar to the above recipe.

BROWN BREAD.

1 c. white flour, 1 c. molasses,
2 c. graham flour, 3½ c. milk,
2 c. Indian meal, pinch salt,
2 tsp. Rumford baking powder.

Beat well before adding baking powder; steam 4 hrs.; dry in the oven 15 min. before serving, after taking from the mould.

BREAD.

1 qt. lukewarm water,
2 tsp. butter, 2 tsp. sugar,
1 cake yeast, dissolved in 1 c. lukewarm water,
or, 1 c. liquid yeast, 4 tsp. salt,
3 to 4 qts. flour.

Have the water a little hot, melt the butter and let stand until lukewarm; add sugar, salt and yeast; stir in flour until a soft dough; beat well; add more flour until stiff enough to handle; lay on floured board, and knead until smooth and elastic, or until the dough springs back into place when pressed with the finger; put back into bowl and let raise until, when pressed by the finger does not spring back into place. Knead the second time, put into pans, let raise until double bulk. Bake 1 hr.

ROLLS.

1 qt. flour, 1-3 cake yeast,
1 tsp. salt, 1 tbsp. sugar,
1 c. boiled milk, 1 tbsp. butter.

Dissolve the yeast in ½ c. lukewarm water, or use ½ c. liquid yeast, and add the yeast, sugar, salt, milk (cooled), and butter. Beat well, set in a warm place. When light, beat again, using a little more flour; let rise. When light, cut through and through, and set in a cool place. When very cold put flour on board and roll out and cut in rounds. Put a small piece of butter on each, fold over and let rise. Bake quick.

AMERICAN BUNS.

1½ c. milk, 1 cake yeast, 1½ c. sugar,
Flour enough to make a stiff batter,
½ c. butter, ½ tsp. soda.

Dissolve the yeast in ½ c. lukewarm water, and add to the milk, also the 1 c. sugar. Let rise over night; in the morning add the rest of the sugar, butter and soda. Flour enough to make as stiff as bread. After second raising, add a small c. currants. Cut out and put in pans, until twice their size. Bake.

TURN-OVER ROLLS.

Scald 1 qt. milk, and add to it ½ c. sugar, ½ c. butter, 1 tsp. salt, and enough flour to make a batter as thick as for pancakes. Let it cool, and when lukewarm stir in a ½ c. liquid yeast, or 1 cake dissolved in a little warm water. (1 c.). Set in a warm place to rise, and when very light, ad'd flour and knead into a dough, not too stiff, flatten with a rolling-pin, and cut into cakes about an inch thick, with a biscuit-cutter. Roll out each cake, spread with butter, fold, let rise again. Bake 25 min.

FRENCH ROLLS.

These rolls are made from raised bread dough,—that is, after the first rising. Roll a piece of dough until half an inch thick, and 10 or 12 inches square. Spread with a tsp. soft butter; sprinkle with 4 level tbsp. sugar, a little cinnamon. Now, roll up, like a jelly roll, and pinch the edges tight down. Cut in slices an inch or less in width, place on buttered pans, raise again, and let bake. Serve cold.

GINGER BREAD.

1½ c. molasses, ¾ c. drippings,
1 tsp. ginger, 1 tsp. soda,
1½ c. boiling water,
Flour enough to make a very stiff batter.

Mix all together, and then thin with the boiling water. You will find it thin, but that is the way it should be. Bake from 30 to 45 min.

BRIOCHE PASTE.

For two large loaves there will be required
1 qt. flour, 1 generous c. butter,
½ c. of water, 1 tbsp. sugar, 1 tsp. salt,
½ cake of compressed yeast,
8 small, or 7 large eggs.

Dissolve the yeast in the water, which should be lukewarm. Put some boiling water in a bowl and let it stand for 5 min., then pour out the water, wipe the bowl dry, and put 1 c. flour into it; add the dissolved yeast to the flour, and beat well. Cover the bowl and set in a warm place until the mixture rises to double its size. About half an hour after the sponge has been set, put the remainder of the flour, salt, sugar, butter and 3 of the eggs in a large bowl, mix the ingredients well with the hand, and when a smooth paste is formed, add the remainder of the eggs, one at a time, beating the paste vigorously until it is very light and smooth. The eggs should not be beaten before they are added. Now, if the sponge be raised, add it to the paste, and beat well; should it not be raised enough, it will not hurt the beaten mixture to stand awhile. When the sponge is thoroughly incorporated with the paste, cover the bowl and set in a warm place. It will take about 6 hrs. for the sponge to rise sufficiently. When it becomes light, beat well and then put it on or beside the ice. Let it remain there for 10 or 12 hrs., and it will then be ready for use. The sponge may be set at 2 o'clock in the afternoon, and be ready to add to the paste at 3. The paste will be ready to put on the ice at 9, and it the morning will be ready to use in any form.

BABA BREAD.

To make a large loaf of baba, use 3 c. of paste, ½ c. currants, 1 c. raisins, and ½ c. wine. Soak the fruit in the wine over night. In the morning, work the fruit and wine into the paste. Butter a deep mould, and put the paste into it. Cover and put in a warm place to rise to twice its original size. It will take about an hour and a half. Bake in a moderate oven from 40 to 50 min. On taking from the oven, turn from the mould on a deep plate or dish, the top of the bread being down. Let it cool in this position. While the bread is cooling, make a syrup by boiling together for 12 min., 1 c. sugar and ¾ c. water. At the end of the time add 4 tbsp. rum to the syrup, and pour the liquid over the bread or cake (which we will call it serving as a dessert), being careful to wet the sides with it. Let the bread and syrup get perfectly cold, and serve as a dessert.

SMALL CAKES.

COOKIES.

1 c. butter, 2 eggs,
2 c. sugar, ½ c. sweet milk,
2 tsp. Rumford baking powder.
Flavor to taste, flour enough to roll.

GINGER SNAPS.

1 c. sugar, 1 c. butter,
1 c. molasses, 1 tbsp. soda,
6 tbsp. cold water, spices to taste,
Flour enough to handle.

LOVE CAKES.

2 c. sugar, 1 c. butter,
Flour enough to roll, 4 eggs.

Roll very thin; before baking sprinkle on each cake a little granulated sugar.

CREAM PUFFS.

3 eggs, 1 c. boiling water,
½ c. butter, 1 c. flour, ½ tsp. soda.

Melt the butter in the boiling water; add flour and soda, which have been sifted together; stir until smooth and thick; remove from the fire, cool a little, then add the eggs, one at a time, and beat about 3 min. Do not beat eggs before adding to the mixture. Allow 1 hp. tbsp. for each puff; bake on a greased pan (butter) in a moderate oven. Bake about ½ hr. to ¾ hr. Fill with a cream made from

1 c. milk, 1 egg, ½ c. sugar,
¼ c. flour, vanilla.

SUGAR CAKES.

3 eggs, 1 c. butter,
2 c. sugar, 1 c. milk,
2 tsp. Rumford baking powder,
Flour to roll, 1 tsp. vanilla.
Be careful not to make them too stiff.

CRULLERS.

2 large c. sugar, 3 eggs,
1 pt. sweet milk, butter size walnut,
2 tsp. Rumford baking powder,
1 nutmeg, grated, and flour enough to make a very soft dough.

SPICE CAKES.

1 c. brown sugar, ½ c. butter,
1 c. sour cream, or milk,
4 c. flour, 1 tsp. soda,
4 eggs, 1 tsp. cloves,
1 tsp. cinnamon, 1 tsp. allspice,
1 lb. raisins, seeded.
Mix according to rule, and drop by the spoon.

DROP SUGAR CAKES.

2 c. sugar, 3 eggs,
½ c. butter, 1 c. sour milk,
1 tsp. soda, 2 tsp. cream of tartar,
Flavor to taste.
Flour enough to drop with a spoon.

TAYLOR CAKES, No. 1.

Melt 1 c. butter or lard, and add it to 2 c. molasses, 1 c. buttermilk, 1 tbsp. soda, 2 tbsp. ginger, 3 eggs, and flour enough to drop off a spoon.

TAYLOR CAKES, No. 2.

1 c. sugar, 1 c. butter,
4 eggs, 1 c. buttermilk,
2 c. molasses, 2 tbsp. cinnamon,
2 tsp. soda, 8 c. flour.

Mix 1 tsp. soda with the milk, the other with the molasses; pour together and warm; add eggs, well beaten, then the other ingredients.

PEPPER NUTS.

1 c. butter, 2 c. sugar,
4 eggs, ½ c. milk,
1 tsp. soda, flavor with mace and rose water,
Flour enough to roll.

A. P's.

1 qt. flour, 2 c. sugar,
½ c. butter, ½ c. lard,
1 large nutmeg, grated,
1 scant tsp. soda, 1 c. cold water.

Mix as for pastry, roll thin, cut in shape with a knife. Bake brown. The longer these are kept the better they are.

GINGER COOKIES.

1 c. milk or water, 2 c. molasses,
1 c. butter or lard, 1½ tsp. soda,
1 tsp. ginger, ½ tsp. cinnamon.

Mix together, add enough flour to handle, roll thin, cut and cook until brown, in a quick oven.

Mix the flour and sugar; add to the egg, pour on the boiling milk; mix well, return to the boiler and cook 10 min., stirring all the time. When cool, flavor. When ready, make a small opening in the side of the puff and fill with the cream. This amount will be enough for ten or twelve puffs.

SAND TARTS.

1 c. butter, 1½ c. sugar,
3 eggs, (separate), 1 tbsp. water,
½ tsp. Rumford baking powder.

Mix all together and add enough flour to handle; roll out thin and cut in squares, sprinkle cinnamon and sugar on top, and bake until brown in a moderate oven.

COCOANUT SNAPS.

1 lb. brown sugar, 1 c. molasses,
½ c. butter, 3 c. flour,
Scant ½ c. prepared cocoanut, or
½ cocoanut, grated.

Mix all together, roll out thin as a wafer; bake in a moderate oven until brown. These cakes will keep several days in a cool place before baking, and the longer they are kept after baking the better they are.

MACAROONS.

1 lb. almonds, 2 tsp. rose water.
Whites of 5 eggs, 1 c. powdered sugar.
1 tsp. almond essence, 3 tbsp. flour.

Beat the whites until stiff, add sugar and flour; add carefully. Blanch, dry and pound the almonds to a paste, using the rose water; add to the eggs, also the essence. Roll into small balls, place on buttered paper, some distance apart. Bake slowly until brown.

LADY FINGERS.

4 eggs, ½ c. pulverized sugar.
Pinch salt, 1 tsp. vanilla, ¾ c. flour.

Separate eggs, beat yolks until thick and creamy, add sugar, gradually, also salt and vanilla; beat the whites until stiff, add to the yolks, alternate with the flour. Do not beat. When well mixed, put in lady finger pans, or drop off a tablespoon into a buttered pan. Sprinkle a little powdered sugar on top, and bake about 15 min. in a moderate oven.

COCOANUT DROPS.

1 cocoanut, grated; its weight in granulated sugar, ½ c. flour, and white of 1 egg. Beat the whites stiff and add the other ingredients. Shape into balls and bake from 20 to 25 min., or until brown.

JELLIED COOKIES.

2 eggs, 1 c. sugar, ½ c. cold water,
Scant 1½ c. flour, 1 tsp. vanilla,
1 tsp. Rumford baking powder.

Separate the eggs, and beat the yolks until creamy; add sugar, beat well, flavor, pour in water and flour, alternately, (in which the baking powder has been sifted), and lastly fold in the whites, beaten stiff. Bake the same as for "Chocolate Squares." Put jelly between and dip in either chocolate, caramel or white icing.

VANILLA CAKES.

Cream ½ c. butter and 1½ c. sugar; add 3 eggs beat well, 2 tsp. vanilla; then ½ c. milk, and 2 c. flour. Drop on greased tins, and bake in a hot oven. Wafers may be made by using enough flour, so they can be rolled out thin, cut and bake about 10 or 12 min.

CHOCOLATE SQUARES.

4 hp. tbsp. grated chocolate,
2 tbsp. flour, ¼ tsp. cinnamon,
¼ tsp. Rumford baking powder,
6 eggs, 1 c. pulverized sugar,
Juice and grated rind of ½ lemon.

Mix the flour, chocolate, baking powder, and cinnamon together. Separate the eggs. Add the powdered sugar to the yolks, and beat until very light; then add the rind and juice of the lemon, and beat hard. Add the dry ingredients, and lastly fold in the whites, beaten stiff. Bake in shallow, square cake pans, in a moderate oven, from 20 to 30 min. When the cake is cold, spread either a cream filling or jelly between the layers. Ice with chocolate icing, and when it hardens, cut in squares.

CHOCOLATE CAKES.

½ c. butter, 1 c. sugar, pinch salt, 1 egg.
2 hp. tbsp. grated chocolate, ½ tsp. soda,
2 tbsp. milk, 2½ c. flour.

Cream the butter and sugar, add chocolate, melted; also egg, beat well, then salt and flour; dissolve the soda in the milk, and stir in carefully.

ALMOND CAKES.

1 c. butter, 1 c. sugar, 6 eggs,
2 c. flour, 1 tsp. vanilla, 1 c. almonds.

Cream the butter and sugar, separate the eggs, beat yolks until very creamy, stir into the butter and sugar, beat well, add flavoring, then flour, and lastly the whites, beaten stiff. Chop nuts, not too fine, stir in carefully. Bake in greased muffin-pans. Put a whole almond on the top of each cake before putting in the oven.

GINGER CAKES.

1 c. molasses, ¼ c. butter (melted),
1 c. sugar, ½ c. cold water,
1 tbsp. ginger, ½ tbsp. cinnamon,
1 tsp. soda, 2 tsp. salt,
Flour enough to make a stiff dough.

Cream butter and sugar in a warm bowl, add molasses; when well mixed, stir in the spices, and salt. Dissolve the soda in the water and stir this in. Gradually work in the flour, beating well.

Put a small piece of dough on a floured board and roll thin. Cut and bake in a hot oven.

MOLASSES CAKES.

1 c. molasses, 1 tsp. soda.
¼ c. butter, ½ tsp. cinnamon.
½ tsp. ginger, ½ c. milk.
Pinch salt, flour.

Melt butter in a warm bowl, add molasses and soda, dissolved in a little warm water, stir in spices, salt and milk, and enough flour to make a batter thick enough to drop from a spoon. Bake on greased pan in a moderate oven, about 20 to 25 min.

SPICED CRULLERS.

1 c. sugar, 2 eggs, 2 tbsp. butter, melted.
½ c. milk, ½ tsp. salt, 1 tsp. cinnamon,
1 tsp. nutmeg, ½ tsp. allspice, flour,
2 tsp. baking powder, "Rumford."

Mix according to "Crullers."

PLAIN CAKES FOR CHILDREN.

1-3 c. butter, 1 c. sugar, 1 egg.
1 c. milk, 2 c. flour, pinch salt,
2 tsp. Rumford baking powder.

Cream the butter, and gradually add the sugar; separate the egg; beat the white stiff and the yolk thick and creamy. Stir the milk into the yolk and add it alternately with the flour (into which the baking powder has been sifted), to the butter and sugar. Beat well, flavor with 1 tsp. lemon or vanilla, fold in the white, beaten stiff. Bake in greased muffin-pans, 25 to 30 min. A few raisins or currants may be aded.

DOUGHNUTS MADE WITH LARD.

Beat 2 eggs and 1 c. of sugar together; add 4 tbsp. of melted lard, 1 c. sour milk, 1 tsp. soda, pinch salt, spices to taste, and flour enough to make a soft dough. Roll into shape and fry in a bath of fat.

GINGERBREAD CAKES.

Take a cup and put into it 3 tbsp. of hot water, 3 tbsp. butter, and when the butter is melted, fill the cup up with molasses. Put into a bowl and add 1 tsp. of ginger, ½ tsp. cinnamon, and 1 tsp. soda. Stir in enough flour to make a stiff dough. Pour into square tins and bake carefully. If you have not the square tins, muffin-pans may be used, or a regular gingerbread pan. When perfectly cold, cut into squares. These little cakes are very nice iced with plain frosting.

PIES.

LEMON PIE, No. 1.

1 lemon, rind and juice,
1 c. sugar, 3 tbsp. flour,
1 c. milk, 2 eggs.

Separate the eggs, beat the yolks, and add the sugar, rind, juice and flour, wet in a little of the cold milk; pour on the remainder of the milk, and pour into the pie plates lined with crust. Bake 30 min. Make a meringue of the whites, and 1 tbsp. pulverized sugar, and bake in a moderate oven until a golden brown.

LEMON PIE, No. 2.

2 lemons, rind and juice,
1½ c. sugar, 3 tbsp. cornstarch,
2 c. boiling water, yolks 3 eggs,
Whites 3 eggs, 1 tbsp. pulverized sugar.

Mix the cornstarch and sugar, add the boiling water, cook 5 min., cool a little and add the yolks, well beaten, juice and rind; pour into the crust, and bake according to the length of time for baking pies. Make a meringue of the whites and pulverized sugar, and make the same as for Lemon Pie No. 1.

LEMON PIE, No. 3.

2 lemons, rind and juice,
2 potatoes, size of lemons,
1 tbsp. flour, 1 c. sugar,
Small piece of butter, 2 c. boiling water.
Yolks 3 eggs, whites 3 eggs.

Grate the potatoes and thin with the water; add sugar and

flour, wet with a little cold water; cook 5 min. When cool, add yolks, pour into the pastry, bake. Make a meringue of the whites.

COCOANUT PIE, No. 1.

1 c. cocoanut, 1 pt. milk.
2 tbsp. cornstarch, yolks 3 eggs.
1 tbsp. sugar, pinch salt, 1 tbsp. butter.

Soak the cocoanut in the boiling milk. Blend the cornstarch in a little cold milk, and add to the boiling milk. Separate the eggs, and add the sugar to the well-beaten yolks. Cook the cornstarch 5 min. Just before removing, add the butter. When cool, pour in the yolks, sugar, and salt. Flavor with vanilla or lemon. Make a meringue of the whites.

COCOANUT PIE, No. 2.

3½ c. milk, 5 eggs.
Sweeten to taste.
1 c. cocoanut.

Beat eggs, and pour in milk; add cocoanut, and sugar; pour into pastry, and bake according to time for pies. This will make two pies.

PUMPKIN PIE.

Pare and cut the pumpkin into small pieces, and cook in boiling, salted water, until tender; drain, and mash fine. To 1 qt. pumpkin, add 1 qt. milk, ½ tbsp. butter, 1½ c. sugar, 3 eggs, 2 tsp. cornstarch, (blend with a little milk and 1 tsp. ground ginger). Mix all ingredients together. Fill the pastry, and grate a little nutmeg on top. Bake until the pumpkin is firm when touched with the finger, and brown.

APPLE PIE.

Use 5 apples to one pie. Cut in slices, put into crust, sprinkle with 4 tbsp. sugar, and if dry, add a little water. Bake with an upper crust.

MINCE PIE.

1 c. meat, chopped fine.
2 c. apples, chopped fine.
3½ c. suet, chopped fine.
1 tbsp. ground cloves, 1 tbsp. ground allspice.
1 tbsp. ground cinnamon, 2 c. sweet cider.
1 c. sugar, (brown). Juice and rind 1 lemon.
¼ tsp. salt, 1 c. raisins, 1 c. currants.
½ c. citron, cut fine, 1 c. molasses.

Cook the meat until tender, and let stand until cold. If there is any of the juice that jellies, add it. Add the other ingredients, and it is ready for use. This will keep in a cool place for weeks, if well covered.

CUSTARD PIE.

Beat 4 eggs together, and add 1 qt. milk, pinch salt, ½ c. sugar. Bake in an under crust.

RAISIN PIE.

Soak ½ c. seeded raisins in 1 c. cold water several hrs. Beat 1 egg until light, add 1 c. sugar, 1 tbsp. flour, juice and rind of 1 lemon, also the raisins and water in which they were soaked. Cook until the mixture thickens. Bake in upper and lower crust.

BALTIMORE CREAM PIE.

Pie,—
2 eggs, 1 c. sugar, 2 c. flour.
1 c. milk, 2 tsp. Rumford baking powder.

Mix the flour and sugar together, add eggs and milk, and lastly the baking powder. Bake in two layers.

Cream,—
2 eggs, 2 c. milk, 4 tsp. sugar.
4 tsp. flour, flavor with vanilla.

Make a custard of the ingredients, and put between the layers of the pie.

ORANGE PIE.

Separate 3 eggs, beat the yolks until creamy, and add 1 c. sugar, 1 tbsp. butter, melted, juice of 2 oranges, and the rind of ½ orange, and 1 c. milk. Bake in lower pie crust. Make a meringue of the whites, and 3 tbsp. powdered sugar.

CRANBERRY PIE.

1 c. cranberries, ½ c. seeded raisins, 1 c. sugar, 1 tbsp. flour, 1 c. water, 1 tsp. vanilla, pinch salt. Mix all together, and bake in a lower and upper crust.

PIE CRUST.

1½ c. flour, 1 hp. tbsp. butter,
¼ tsp. salt, 1 hp. tbsp. lard,
Generous ¼ c. cold water.

Mix the flour and salt together, work in the shortening with the tips of the fingers until sandy. Stir in the cold water with a knife to make a stiff dough. Roll out to fit the pie pan. Handle and use as little extra flour as possible.

WHIPPED CREAM PIE.

Bake 2 lower crusts, until done. Whip 1 generous pt. of cream, and 4 tbsp. sugar, flavor with strawberry or vanilla. Pour into the crusts and dot with sour jelly. Serve.

BANANA PIE.

Line a plate with pastry. Cut four bananas into slices, and put in the crust, sprinkle with sugar, also small pieces of pineapple. Cover with an upper crust and bake from ½ to ¾ hr.

DRIED PEACH PIE.

Soak ½ lb. peaches over night. In the morning pour off any

water that may be on the peaches, put peaches into a sauce-pan with enough cold water to cover them. Simmer slowly until the peaches are tender. Be careful that they do not burn. Five min. before removing from the fire, add 1 tbsp. lemon juice and ½ c. sugar. If not sweet enough, add a little more. Line pie-pan, put in peaches, bake with an upper crust, the length of time for pies.

JELLY TARTS.

Mix enough pastry for a pie, roll out into sheets ½ inch thick, and cut into strips 4 in. by 3½. Bake in a quick oven. When cold, spread ½ the strips with currant or, in fact, any jelly. Lay the other half on top. Serve with frosting, or without.

CREAM PIE.

Scald 2 c. cream in a double boiler. Separate 4 eggs; beat the yolks until creamy; add ½ c. sugar and 1 tbsp. flour; pour over the hot milk, return to the boiler, and cook until thick. Flavor with ½ tsp. vanilla. Line a pie-pan with puff paste, bake, then pour in the cream, make a meringue of the whites, and 1 tbsp. powdered sugar, and bake in a moderate oven until a golden brown. Milk may be used instead of cream. This will make 1 large, or 2 small pies.

STRAWBERRY PIE.

Bake carefully the pie crust. When cold, fill with sugared strawberries, and cover with whipped cream.

MOCK MINCE PIE.

Roll 4 large soda crackers fine and add them to 1 egg, well-beaten. Mix well, then stir in ½ c. molasses, ¼ c. vinegar, ½ c. strong tea, 1 c. chopped raisins, 1 tbsp. butter, 1 tsp. mixed spices and a pinch salt. Bake in a lower and upper crust.

CHOCOLATE PIES.

Put 1 c. milk in a double boiler. Beat the yolks of two eggs, light; add to them 4 tbsp. pulverized sugar, and 1 level tbsp. flour. Pour on this mixture the scaided milk, stir, return to boiler, beating all the time. Add pinch salt; cook 15 min.; take from the fire and stir in 2 hp. tbsp. grated chocolate, melted; mix well. When cold, flavor with 1 tsp. vanilla. Make 2 pastry shells; bake, remove from the oven, pour in the custard. Make a meringue of the whites, and 1 tbsp. pulverized sugar, spread on the pie, and set in a moderate oven until a golden brown.

CHOCOLATE CREAM PIES.

Make 2 lower pie crusts, from puff paste; bake and set away until perfectly cold. Whip 1 pt. cream until thick; sprinkle over ½ c. pulverized sugar. Melt 1 hp. tbsp. chocolate in 4 tbsp. milk and 1½ tbsp. sugar; stir into the whipped cream; stir a few min. Before making the cream, pack an ice-cream freezer solidly with salt and ice, leaving out the paddle. If you have a round mould, pack it in a bucket, instead of using the freezer. Let stand in mould or freezer 4 or 5 hrs without stirring. Be sure and cover the top of mould or freezer with ice; then wet a piece of carpet and cover the top. When ready to serve, take the mould from the ice, dip it in lukewarm water, and turn into the pastry shells. Serve on cold plates, which have been in the ice box several hrs. If you have neither mould or freezer, use a granite and wooden buckets.

Cold Meats and Sauces.

TUMBLE OF COLD MEAT.

3 c. meat, 1 c. soft bread crumbs.
3 tbsp. butter, 3 eggs,
1 c. stock, or milk, 1 tsp. salt,
¼ tsp. pepper, 1 tbsp. onion juice,
1 tbsp. chopped parsley,
1 tbsp. worcestershire sauce.

Chop the meat, add the other ingredients, mix well, bake in buttered cups or dish. Place in a pan of warm water and cover with a piece of greased paper. Cook 1 hr. 15 min. before done, remove the paper and let brown. Serve with brown sauce.

SCALLOPED MEAT.

Scallope,—
2 c. bread crumbs, 1 tbsp. butter,
¼ tsp. salt, pinch pepper.

Gravy,—
1 tbsp. butter, or beef drippings,
1 tbsp. flour, 1 c. stock,
1 tbsp. chopped parsley, 1 tsp. onion juice,
2 tsp. Worcestershire sauce.

Part First—Melt the butter, add bread crumbs and seasoning. Part Second—Melt the butter, add flour and brown; thin with the stock, season, chop 2 c. meat, add parsley, onion juice and a little salt. Spread in the bottom of a buttered baking dish, 1-3 of the bread crumbs, ½ the meat and gravy, then ½ the remainder of the crumbs, all the meat and gravy, and the rest of the crumbs, for a crust. Bake in a hot oven from 20 to 25 min., or until brown.

WARMED-OVER CHICKEN, TURKEY, ETC.

Cut the cold fowl into small pieces; make a sauce by melting 1 tbsp. butter, adding 1 tbsp. flour, thin with 1 c. milk, season, cut 1 can mushrooms in small pieces, add to the sauce, also the liquor; put part of the meat into a buttered baking dish, pour on a little of the sauce, continue so doing until all the meat and sauce are in the dish. (If desired, add a little chopped parsley), and make a covering of buttered crumbs, and brown in a hot oven. If there is any gravy left from the fowl, use it instead of the sauce.

COMPOTE OF COLD MEAT.

2 c. chopped meat, (any kind),
2 eggs, 1 tsp. salt,
3 slices of soft bread,
1 tsp. butter, celery.

Chop the meat, and if any gravy, put all into the sauce-pan; if not gravy, cover the meat with water and add butter. When it has cooked 10 min., add eggs, well-beaten, bread and seasoning, and let come to a boil. Serve at once. If the celery is desired, chop and cook with the meat. This is a nice recipe for any or all kinds of cold cooked meat.

CHICKEN OR VEAL CROQUETTES.

1 pt. chopped veal or chicken,
1 tsp. salt, ¼ tsp. pepper,
1 c. stock or milk, 1 tsp. flour,
1 tsp. onion juice, 1 tbsp. lemon juice,
2 eggs, 1 tbsp. flour, 3 tbsp. butter.

Put stock or milk on to boil; blend flour and butter; add to the boiling stock; cook 2 min; add eggs, well beaten; add the seasoning, lemon juice and onion juice to the meat; stir into the boiling mixture; mix well. Take away from the fire; when cold, shape, roll in crumbs, beaten eggs and crumbs. Fry in a bath of fat.

SWEETBREAD CROQUETTES.

Boil in salt water two pairs of sweetbreads, 20 min. When done, throw into cold water for a few min.; then blanch them (remove the skin); cut into small pieces; also 1 can mushrooms. Melt 1 large tbsp. butter in a sauce-pan, add 1 tbsp. flour, and thin with ½ c. cream, or stock; add sweetbreads and mushrooms. Heat well, and add 2 eggs. Mix and remove from the fire. When cold, form into croquettes, the same as for veal croquettes. Serve both kinds of croquettes with peas.

OYSTER CROQUETTES.

Heat 1 pt. of oysters in their liquor. When they come to a boil remove them from the fire and when cold chop fine. Melt 1 tbsp. butter and add to it 1 hp. tbsp. flour; thin with 1 c. oyster liquor. Cook for 5 min., stirring all the time. Add seasoning, 1 tbsp. chopped parsley, and 2 eggs, stir and cook 3 min. Set away to cool. If too soft to handle, take a small portion from the mixture with a spoon, dip into beaten egg and then into bread crumbs. Fry in a bath of fat.

SCRAMBLED BEEF.

Chop fine 1 c. lean beef; put in a pan with salt, pepper, 1 tbsp. water, ¼ c. rich cream, 1 tbsp. butter, 1 egg. Cook 2 min., stirring constantly. Add 1 tbsp. cracker dust. Serve on squares of toast.

COLD MEAT CRUST PATTIES.

Cut a loaf of bread in slices 1 inch thick, with a pattie cutter; press out as many pieces as you wish patties, and with a small cutter cut half-way through the center. Fry the bread patties in smoking hot fat half a min. Remove, drain, take out the center piece, remove all the soft bread, then fill, and, if desired, put on the centers. Fill with a cream made by melting 2 tbsp. butter, add 1 tbsp. flour, salt and pepper; thin with 1 c. stock; boil a few min., stir in 1 pt. veal, or any cold cooked meat, chopped fine. Add a little lemon juice, and, if desired, a little onion juice. Fill patties. Serve hot.

SWEETBREAD PATTIES.

Boil the sweetbreads until tender. Chop in small pieces. Melt 2 hp. tbsp. butter, put in the sweetbreads, and fry brown. Add 1 can mushrooms, (not the liquor), cut in halves, also 1 tbsp. flour, and slowly 1 pt. boiling cream. Let simmer until smooth and thick. Serve in either pattie shells, or in crust patties.

DEVILED HAM.

1 c. chopped ham, 2 hard boiled eggs.
4 tbsp. milk, 2 tsp. vinegar,
spk. cayenne, pinch mustard, 1 tbsp. butter.

Cream the yolks of eggs with the vinegar and milk; add butter, melted, cayenne and mustard. Mix all together; add chopped whites. Will keep in a dry, cool place several days. This is nice for sandwiches.

SCALLOPED CALVES' BRAINS.

2 set calves' brains, 2 c. bread crumbs,
3 tbsp. butter, 1 pt. milk, salt and pepper.

Wash and separate brains. Cook in boiling water 10 min. Chop in small pieces. Melt butter and mix with crumbs; put in a layer of crumbs in a baking dish; then half the brains, part of the milk; then seasoning, half the remainder of the crumbs, the rest of the brains, and all of the milk. Season and make a top crust of the crumbs. Bake in a hot oven from 20 to 30 min. Serve with Egg Sauce.

DRAWN BUTTER SAUCE.

½ c. butter blended with 2 tbsp. flour, put into sauce-pan with 1 c. boiling water, stirring constantly, until it has cooked 3 min. Just before serving, add 1 tbsp. chopped parsley.

EGG SAUCE.

To Drawn Butter Sauce, add 3 hard cooked eggs, chopped.

MINT SAUCE.

½ c. vinegar, 4 tbsp. mint, 2 tbsp. sugar.

Mix together and let stand for an hour or more; strain or serve with the mint in it. Serve with lamb.

CURRANT SAUCE.

1 tbsp. butter, 1 hp. tbsp. flour.
1 c. stock, or milk, salt and pepper.
1 glass currant jelly.

Melt the butter, add flour, grate 1 onion, and cook with the butter 5 min., stir in the milk, season, add jelly, and let melt. Serve with lamb.

TOMATO SAUCE.

1 qt. tomatoes, 2 tbsp. butter, 2 tbsp. flour,
2 cloves, and 1 slice onion.

Cook tomatoes, onions and cloves 10 min. Melt the butter, add the flour. When smooth and browned, stir in the tomatoes. Cook 10 min. Season to taste, and run through a strainer. Serve with fish, meat or macaroni.

BROWN SAUCE.

Melt 1 tbsp. butter, add 1 tsp. onion juice and 1 tbsp. flour. Cook until brown; thin with either 1 c. stock or 1 c. milk. Season. Cook 5 min. Serve with meat, fish or game.

HOLLANDAISE SAUCE.

Cream ½ c. butter, add the yolks 2 eggs, and beat well; stir in the juice of ½ lemon, ½ tsp. salt and pinch cayenne. When ready to serve, add ½ c. boiling water. Set over the tea-kettle, and cook until like soft custard. Stir all the time. Serve with fish.

WHITE SAUCE.
1 tbsp. butter, 1 c. veal stock.
1 tbsp. flour, ¼ tsp. salt, pinch pepper.

Melt the butter, and as soon as it bubbles, add the flour and seasoning; stir in the stock. Cook 5 min. Serve with meats.

Desserts, Ice Creams and Sherberts.

FRIED APPLES.

Wash, pare and quarter as many apples as desired; melt butter in a frying-pan, just the same as for frying vegetables; put in apples and let fry about 15 min.; slowly, then, add to 1 qt. apples, 4 tbsp. sugar. Serve hot, with cream and sugar, or as a vegetable.

BANANAS AND WHIPPED CREAM.

Peel and slice ½ doz. bananas into thin slices; sprinkle with 2 tbsp. pulverized sugar; put in a pretty glass dish; set on ice. Serve with whipped cream.

WINE JELLY.

Soak 1 box gelatine in 1 c. cold water, 2 hrs. Dissolve by pouring 2 c. boiling water over the gelatine; then add the juice of 1 lemon, 2 c. sugar, and 2 c. sherry wine; stir until all is dissolved. Strain through a napkin, pour into a mould, and place on ice for 6 or 8 hrs.

PINEAPPLE SMOTHERED IN STRAWBERRIES.

Pare and remove the eyes from one fresh pineapple; tear into small pieces with a silver fork; pick and wash two baskets of strawberries. In a pretty dish make a layer of berries, then pineapple, and so on. Be sure and have the top layer strawberries. Sprinkle each layer with pulverized sugar. Serve with fruit juice sauce, using strawberry juice, and omit the butter. Let the syrup stand until perfectly cold before using.

PEACHES AND WHIPPED CREAM.

Peaches should be pared and cut in halves. Arrange them in a pretty dish, and sprinkle with pulverized sugar, not more than 3 tbsp. to two dozen peaches. Serve at once, as they become dark if allowed to stand long after being pared. They should be put on ice before being pared and cut. Serve with whipped cream. Apricots are served the same way as peaches.

CHOCOLATE MOUSSE.

Pack a freezer or mould with ice and salt. Whip 1 qt. cream until thick. Put in a small sauce-pan, 1 hp. tbsp. grated chocolate, 3 tbsp. sugar, 1 tbsp. boiling water, and stir over the fire until smooth and glossy. Add ¼ c. of cream. Sift 1 c. pulverized sugar over the whipped cream. Pour on the chocolate, slowly, and stir gently until well mixed with the cream, and turn into the freezer (without the paddle), or mould. Cover, put ice on top. Cover with a piece of carpet. Stand to one side for 4 or 5 hrs. Turn out on steak platter when ready to use.

CHERRY SHERBET.

Boil 1 qt. of water and 1 lb. granulated sugar, 15 min. Stone 1 qt. cherries, and cut into quarters, and add to the syrup. Let stand until perfectly cold. Press through a fine sieve and freeze.

ROMAN PUNCH.

Make a lemonade of 4 large, juicy lemons, 1 qt. water, and 2½ c. granulated sugar. Beat 4 eggs (whites), until very stiff; add 4 tbsp. pulverized sugar to them; beat again. Partly freeze the lemonade, then pour the eggs, 2 tbsp. rum, ½ c. champagne, into it. Repack, freeze until firm. No not stir.

VANILLA ICE CREAM.

1 qt. cream, 2 tsp. vanilla,
Generous ½ c. sugar.

Mix all together; freeze.

APPLE SHERBET.

Put 1 lb. sugar, 4 c. cold water and the grated rind of 1 lemon on to boil. Pare and core 1 qt. apples, and put on in the syrup. Cook until the apples are very soft; mash through a fine sieve. Add the juice of the lemons, and when perfectly cold, whites of 2 eggs, beaten stiff. Freeze the same as for Cherry Sherbet.

CARAMEL ICE CREAM.

1 pt. milk (scalded), 2 eggs, 2 c. sugar,
1-3 c. flour, scant; 1 qt. cream.

Mix 1 c. sugar and flour together, add eggs, beat well, pour the milk, return to the boiler, and cook about 15 or 20 min. Melt the other c. sugar in a sauce-pan, stirring all the time; be careful not to burn it. When melted, add to the custard, stir while pouring. When cool, thin with the cream. The custard makes a nice foundation for any kind of cream.

CHOCOLATE ICE CREAM.

1 c. milk, 3 eggs,
6 tbsp. grated chocolate,
1 pt. cream, sugar.

Mix the chocolate and milk, put in the top part of the double boiler, and cook until the chocolate is melted. Beat the eggs, add the hot milk, return to the boiler, and cook 2 minutes. Sweeten to taste, make very sweet. When cold, add cream and freeze.

STRAWBERRY ICE CREAM.

1 qt. cream, 2½ c. sugar, 2 qts. strawberries.

Mash the berries, or leave them whole. Put on the sugar, and let stand about 2 hrs. Add cream; if not very sweet, add more sugar, as it will depend upon how sour the berry is, how much sugar will be required. Freeze.

FROZEN BERRIES.

1 qt. berries, 1 qt. cream, 1½ c. sugar.

Make the cream very sweet. Freeze. When nearly hard, remove the paddle, add the berries whole, which have been standing on the ice, with a little sugar on them; stir carefully, but be sure they are well mixed. Cover, and let stand until frozen stiff, about 2 or 3 hrs.

FROZEN LEMON JELLY.

2 tbsp. gelatine, 2 c. cold water,
1 c. boiling water, ½ c. sugar,
¾ c. lemon juice, 2 tbsp. wine.

Soak the gelatine in a little of the cold water, dissolve by pouring on the boiling water, add sugar, lemon juice and wine, if desired. Strain, freeze. Orange may be made the same way, by using orange juice.

FROZEN FRUITS.

1 pt. milk, 1 qt. cream, 6 eggs,
2½ c. sugar, 1 c. chopped peaches, pineapple.
Almonds, green-gages and oranges.

Beat the eggs, add sugar, pour on the boiling milk, mix well. When cool, add cream and fruit. Freeze.

ORANGE SHERBET.

1 qt. milk, 2 c. sugar, juice 14 oranges.

Mix and freeze without cooking.

MILK SHERBET.

1 qt. milk, 2 c. sugar.
Rind of 2 lemons and the juice of 5.
Whites 3 eggs, 1 tbsp. gelatine.

Put the milk, sugar and rind on to boil. Cook 2 or 3 min.

Remove from the fire, strain, and when cool, put into the freezer. When partly frozen, add juice, dissolved gelatine and whites, beaten stiff. Let stand for 3 or 4 hrs.

PINEAPPLE SHERBET.

1 can pineapple, or 1 fruit, 2 c. sugar,
2 c. water, 1 tbsp. gelatine.

Soak the gelatine in enough cold water to cover it, 1 hr. Dissolve in ½ c. boiling water; add the pineapple, sugar and the rest of the water. Freeze as you would creams.

OYSTER SAUCE.

To Drawn Butter Sauce add 1 c. oysters, drained, a few drops of lemon. Let come to a boil. Serve with fish.

LEMON WATER ICE.

1 qt. water, 2 c. sugar, juice 3 large lemons.

Boil the water, sugar and rind 5 min.; then cool and add juice of the lemons. Strain and freeze.

BROWN BREAD ICE CREAM.

Dry 4 slices of brown bread, roll and sift. Whip 1 pt. cream and add to it 1 pt. milk, and 1 c. sugar. Partially freeze; then add the sifted brown bread.

RASPBERRY WHIP.

Soak ½ box gelatine in ½ c. cold water, 1 hr. Dissolve in ½ c. boiling water, add 1 c. sugar and 1 pt. raspberry juice. Strain, and when it begins to form, stir into 1 pt. of cream that has been whipped. Turn into a mould and set on ice.

STRAWBERRY WHIP.

Cut sponge cake in slices and moisten with strawberry juice.

Line a dish with the cake and fill with crushed and sweetened strawberries. Beat the whites of 4 eggs until stiff, add 3 tbsp. pulverized sugar, stir in about 2 tbsp. of the berry juice, beat well. Heap on the berries, and keep cool until ready to serve.

SNOW FLAKE FOAM.

Whip 1 pt. cream; beat the whites of 3 eggs until stiff; add 1 c. sugar, and 1 tsp. vanilla; stir into the cream. Beat all together; pour into a glass dish and set into a bowl of ice to send to the table. Eat with sponge cake.

VELVET SHERBET.

The juice of 6 lemons, and the thinly shaved rind of 2, soaked in the juice ½ hr. Strain and add sugar to make a thick batter, about 5 or 6 c. Add 3 pt. milk. Freeze. Let stand 2 hrs. after frozen.

CHOCOLATE FOAM.

Cook 2 squares of unsweetened chocolate, 4 tbsp. sugar, 4 tbsp. hot water, ¼ tsp. salt, until smooth. Add ½ c. cream, ½ c. milk, and 2 eggs, well beaten. Stir until it thickens. Add ½ tsp. vanilla. Serve cold, with whipped cream.

Jellies, Pickles and Relishes.

STRAWBERRIES AND PINEAPPLES.

1 pt. grated pineapple,
1 pt. strawberries,
1 pt. granulated sugar.

Cook all together 20 min. Jar while hot.

PINEAPPLE MARMALADE.

1 pt. grated pineapple,
1 pt. sugar.

Cook the same as for strawberries and pineapples.

RASPBERRIES AND CURRANTS.

1 c. currant juice,
2 c. raspberries, 2 c. sugar.

Cook the currants in water until tender, strain, then add the raspberries and sugar to the juice and cook 20 min. This will keep in jelly glasses having lids.

STRAWBERRY PRESERVES.

To 1 lb. strawberries use ¾ lb. sugar, put in layers, without water. Place in a kettle on the back of the stove until the sugar is dissolved into a syrup; then let come to a boil, stirring from the bottom. Spread on platters not too thick, and set in the hot sun for two or three days, or until the syrup thickens. Put in tumblers. Strawberries cooked in this way retain their color and flavor.

LEMON BUTTER.

4 eggs, 2 lemons,
½ c. butter, 2 c. sugar.

Separate the eggs; beat the yolks, and add the sugar, butter and lemon juice, and cook in a double boiler until thick; add beaten whites. Serve cold.

PEACH PRESERVE.

2 qts. peaches, 2 qts. sugar.

Wash, pare, stone, peaches; put in sauce-pan and cover with the sugar; set on back of stove until syrup is formed; then let cook slowly about 1 hr. Jar while hot.

FRESH PEACHES.

Wash, pare, stone, free peaches, leaving them in halves; make a syrup of 1 qt. sugar and a generous pt. of water; let cook a few min.; then drop the peaches, a few at a time, into the syrup, and cook until easily pierced with a fork, but not soft. Put into jars, and when full, add a little syrup to cover them. Seal while hot.

CURRANT JELLY.

Wash carefully 6 qts currants; put in a sauce-pan with 2 qts. of water, and cook for ½ hr. or more; strain through cheese cloth. To make the jelly, take 1 qt. syrup and 1 qt. sugar, and cook until it drops thickly from a spoon, when cool. All jellies are made the same way.

TOMATO CATSUP.

½ bu. tomatoes, 1 qt. vinegar,
¼ lb. salt, 1 oz. allspice,
1 oz. cloves, ½ lb. brown sugar,
2 oz. celery seed, 1 tbsp. cayenne,
1 pt. sherry wine, 6 large onions.

Boil the onions and tomatoes until thoroughly cooked; then

strain through a fine sieve. Tie pieces in a bag, add to the juice of the tomatoes, with the salt, pepper, sugar, and vinegar, and cook until thick. Just before bottling, add the wine.

CHILLI SAUCE.

1 pk. ripe tomatoes, 1 qt. sliced onions,
6 green peppers (chopped fine),
½ c. mustard seed, 2 c. brown sugar,
4 tbsp. salt, 1 qt. cider vinegar, 1 tbsp. cloves,
1 tbsp. allspice, 1 tbsp. cinnamon.

Mix all together, using ground spices. Boil 3 hrs. Bottle while hot and seal.

PLUM SAUCE.

1 pk. plums, 1 c. vinegar,
8 lbs. granulated sugar, 1 tbsp. ground allspice,
1 tbsp. ground cinnamon, 1 tbsp. ground cloves.

Mix all ingredients, and boil 1 hr., stirring often. Jar while hot.

STUFFED PEPPERS.

1 doz. green peppers,
1 good-sized head cabbage,
1 bunch celery, ½ doz. small cucumbers,
2 tbsp. mustard seed, vinegar.

Remove seeds from the peppers, keeping tops; put peppers in weak salt water over night; chop cabbage and put in a crock; sprinkle 2 tbsp. salt on top; put plate and weight to cover and let stand over night. In the morning drain off salt water from cabbage, and add the celery and cucumbers, chopped fine; also mustard seed. Drain the peppers well, fill the peppers with this mixture; put on tops, and tie well with white cord. Put in a crock and cover with cold vinegar. They will be ready for use in three weeks. Keep a plate and weight on them, so that the peppers are kept under the vinegar. All that is necessary for a covering for the crocks is a white cloth; tie tight.

BORDEAUX SAUCE.

1 gal. green tomatoes (sliced),
2 gals. cabbage (chopped fine),
1 doz. onions (cut fine),
1 tbsp. tumeric,
1 oz. whole cloves, 1 oz. whole allspice,
1 oz. whole celery seed, ½ lb. mustard seed,
½ c. salt, 1½ lbs. brown sugar, 1 gal. vinegar.

Scald the vinegar, and pour over the other ingredients. This does not require cooking.

CHOW-CHOW, WITH MUSTARD PASTE.

1 qt. LARGE cucumbers, pared and cut in pieces,
1 qt. SMALL cucumbers,
3 pts. small white onions, pared,
1 qt. green tomatoes, sliced,
6 large green peppers, seeds removed,
2 large cauliflower, cut fine,
1 bunch celery, cut in small pieces.

Put all in salt brine over night. In the morning drain, and put in to the mustard paste and cook slightly.

VEGETABLE PICK-UP.

Chop fine ½ doz. green peppers, (remove seeds),
Chop fine 2 red peppers, (remove seeds),
1 pt. small onions,
1 pt. lima beans, (boil until half-done),
1 pt. green corn, (boil 5 min.),
Bunch celery, ½ pk. small string beans,
Cauliflower, or any other vegetable you have to add

Boil ½ gal. cider vinegar, to which has been added ¼ lb. yellow mustard, ¼ lb. mustard seed, ½ lb. white sugar, 2 cts. worth tumeric, and 2 cts. worth celery seed, 5 min;. then add vegetables and cook until tender, an hour or longer.

MUSTARD PASTE.

6 tbsp. ground mustard.
Enough water to make a paste.
1½ c. sugar, 1 c. flour.
1 tbsp. tumeric, 2 qts. cider vinegar.
Mix ingredients, cook slowly until thick, and add pickle.

INVALID COOKERY.

BEEF TEA.

Cut ½ lb. lean, juicy beef in small pieces, and put with 1 c. cold water in a top part of a double boiler, and let stand ½ to 1 hr. Then put boiling water in lower part and cook 20 min. Strain, and season with salt, as used.

BEEF JUICE. No. 1.

Broil a slice of lean beef from the round, a very few min., or until the juice begins to flow. Then squeeze the juice out of the meat by using a meat press.

STEAMED RICE.

2 tbsp. rice, 1 c. milk.
Pinch salt.

Wash the rice well, put with the milk and salt, in a double boiler, and cook from 2 to 3 hrs., stirring once or twice. In case it becomes too dry before done, add a little more milk. Serve with cream and sugar.

IRISH MOSS BLANC MANGE.

2 tbsp. Irish moss, strip lemon peel,
1 pt. milk, pinch salt.

Pick over, wash and soak the moss. Heat the milk in a double boiler, pour off the water in which the moss has been soaked, squeeze the water out, and add to the milk, also the lemon rind, (in case the moss is very salty, do not add the salt).

Cook ½ hr., strain, and set away to cool and harden. Serve with cream and sugar.

POACHED EGG ON TOAST.

Toast 1 slice of bread, dip in boiling salted water, spread with a little butter. Cook 1 egg in boiling, salted water, which must boil. Remove to the back of the stove, put in egg, cook until a film is formed over the yolk; put on toast, season with salt. Serve at once.

MILK TOAST.

½ tbsp. butter, ½ tbsp. flour,
Generous ½ c. milk, pinch salt,
1 small slice toast.

Melt the butter, add flour and salt, and slowly the hot milk. Do not let it lump. Cook 3 to 4 min. Toast the bread over the red-hot coals, if gas is used, over the top of the stove with the lids on. Soften by dipping into boiling milk. Pour the sauce over the toast and serve hot.

WINE JELLY.

½ box gelatine, ½ c. cold water,
1 c. boiling water, ½ c. sugar, ½ c. wine.

Soak the gelatine in the cold water 1 hr. Add boiling water, sugar and wine, stir until sugar is dissolved. Strain through a fine cloth. Keep on ice until hard. Cut in squares, serve on a saucer, with or without a little cream.

ORANGE JELLY.

½ box gelatine, ½ c. cold water,
½ c. boiling water, ½ c. sugar,
Juice of ½ lemon, 1 c. orange juice.

Soak the gelatine in the cold water; add boiling water, lemon and orange juice, and also sugar. Stir until dissolved; strain. Harden.

LEMON JELLY.

¼ box gelatine, ¼ c. cold water,
½ c. boiling water, ½ c. sugar,
¼ c. lemon juice, small piece of stick cinnamon.

Soak the gelatine in cold water; steep the cinnamon in the boiling water 10 min.; pour over gelatine; add the other ingredients, and stir until dissolved; strain.

CALVES' FOOT BROTH.

2 calves' feet, 1 qt. cold water.
2-3 glass white wine,
1 tsp. of the jelly, pinch nutmeg.
A little sugar, yolk 1 egg,
1 tsp. butter, lemon peel.

Cook the calves' feet in the water until 1 pt.; strain and set away for use. When required to make the broth, add the wine to the tsp. of jelly. Be sure to remove the fat. Put the jelly, wine, sugar, and nutmeg in a sauce-pan. When it boils, add a little to the yolk, add the butter, stir well; do not put it on the stove again. The lemon peel may be omitted.

ARROWROOT JELLY.

Place 1 c. of water, a glass of sherry, a little grated nutmeg, and 1 tbsp. fine sugar in a baking dish, and when it boils, add, gradually, 1 tbsp. arrowroot, which has been rubbed smooth in 1 tbsp. of cold water. Boil all together 5 min., stirring all the time. Pour into glasses. Set away to cool. Flavor with either orange or lemon.

ARROWROOT CUSTARD.

Mix 1 tbsp. powdered arrowroot with 3 tbsp. of cold milk; pour on enough boiling milk to make a thin custard. Cook a few min.; cool, then add the well-beaten yolk of 1 egg, and a little sugar. Cook 10 min. in a double boiler.

CUP CUSTARDS.

½ c. milk, pinch salt, 1 egg,
Nutmeg, 2 level tbsp. sugar.

Scald the milk, beat the egg, add sugar and salt, pour on the hot milk, slowly, stirring constantly; bake in cups; grate a little nutmeg on top. Set in a pan, half-filled with boiling water, and bake in a moderate heat. Test with a knife blade, and when it comes out clean they are done.

CREAM OF RICE SOUP.

½ c. stock, (chicken, beef or lamb),
½ c. cream or milk, 1 tbsp. rice, ¼ tsp. salt.

Wash the rice and put in a sauce-pan, with the stock. Cover and put on the back part of the stove, where it will simmer 1 hr. Rub through a fine sieve. Return to the sauce-pan, add cream, re-heat, season as used. You may like a little onion or celery cooked with the rice.

BAKED EGGS.

Separate the eggs; be careful not to break the yolks. Beat the whites, with a pinch of salt, until stiff. Lay on a plate a slice of softened and buttered toast, put the beaten white upon it, drop the yolk in the center and bake a golden brown; or do not separate, but put into a buttered dish and cook until the albumen is firm.

WATERED TOAST.

Put 1 c. boiling water and ½ tsp. salt into a shallow dish, on the back of the stove. Dip a slice of toast in quickly, lay on a hot dish, and butter.

OYSTERS ON TOAST.

Heat ½ c. oysters in their own liquor; skim, and then add 1 tsp. butter and salt to season. Pour the oysters and liquor over a slice of toast, and serve at once.

STEAMED OYSTERS.

Place 5 or 6 oysters, either in the top part of a double boiler or in a saucer over steam. Cook about 3 or 4 min., or until the oyster curls around the edges. Season with salt and a little piece of butter on toasted crackers.

OYSTER STEW.

½ c. oysters, ½ c. milk,
1 tsp. butter, ¼ tsp. salt.

Scald the milk with the salt, add butter. Heat the oysters in a separate pan, and when they puff in the center and curl on the edges, pour the milk over them. Serve at once. Also use the liquor, but strain.

FROZEN BEEF TEA.

Put a small pail in a wooden bucket, and surround it with salt and ice. Be careful, and do not get any salt in the pail. Put cold beef tea into the pail, let stand about 10 min.; remove lid, scrape from the sides; beat well; put on the cover. Continue so doing three or four times, or until frozen smooth. This is for patients that must have their food cold.

JELLIED CHICKEN.

Remove fat and skin from the chicken. Disjoint, put into a sauce-pan with 2 qts. of cold water. Heat slowly, and keep skimming. Simmer for 4 or 5 hrs. Season with salt. Strain; set away to cool. When cold, skim off the fat. Serve as jelly, or heat and serve as soup.

BAKED APPLES, No. 1.

Wash, core and pare sour apples; place on an earthen plate, and in the center of each fill with sugar; pour 1 tbsp. of water to each apple around it, not over it. Bake from 20 to 45 min., or until soft. Serve with rolled oats.

ROLLED OATS.

¾ c. boiling water, ¼ tsp. salt, ¼ c. rolled oats.

Put salt and oats in top part of double boiler, pour on water, steam 1 hr. Serve with cream and sugar, or baked fruit.

A CUTLET.

Cut a lamb cutlet thin, remove all fat and put into a stew-pan with 2 c. water, stick celery, and salt to taste. Let simmer for 2 hrs., or until all the water is cooked away. Serve hot.

BAKED FISH.

Wash and scrape a very small fish, remove eyes, take 2 tbsp. soft bread crumbs, a little onion juice, parsley and salt, mix well; add 1 level tsp. butter, melted, moisten with milk; stuff fish, wipe dry, sprinkle with salt, bake in milk, baste often; cook until tender. Make a sauce by melting 1 tsp. butter, add 1 tsp. flour, pinch salt, thin with the milk in which the fish was cooked.

CREAM OF MUTTON BROTH.

Place 1 c. mutton broth in a sauce-pan. Mix with the yolk of 1 egg, 3 tbsp. of cream or milk; add slowly the boiling broth to the yolk; stir. Serve with squares of toast.

CRACKER GRUEL.

1 tbsp. powdered crackers,

¼ c. boiling water,

¼ c. milk, pinch salt.

Mix the salt with the crackers, add the water and milk; cook for a few min.; strain; add more salt, if needed.

MILK PORRIDGE.

½ doz. raisins, ½ c. milk, 1 tbsp. boiling water,

Pinch salt, ¼ tbsp. flour.

Seed the raisins and cut in small pieces. Add the water and

cook until the water has boiled away. Add the milk and salt. Blend the flour with a little cold milk, and pour into the boiling mixture, stirring constantly. Cook 3 or 4 min. Serve hot. Figs may be used instead of raisins.

RHUBARB WATER.

1 small stock rhubarb.
½ c. boiling water, sugar.

Wash the rhubarb, cut in small pieces, put in a bowl, pour on the water. When cold, strain, sweeten. Serve with chipped ice.

LEMONADE.

1 small or ½ large lemon.
1 c. boiling water.
2 hp. tbsp sugar.

Squeeze the juice into the water, sweeten. If cold lemonade is desired, use cold water instead.

EGG-NOG.

1 egg, 1 tbsp. sugar.
1 tbsp. brandy, 1 c. milk, nutmeg.

Beat the whites until stiff, add the sugar and beat in the yolk and brandy. Pour in milk, and if desired, a little nutmeg. Serve at once. Wine or rum may be used instead of brandy.

ICE CREAM.

1 c. cream, 1 level tbsp. melted chocolate, or
4 tsp. sugar, or 1 tbsp. strawberries.

Mix the sugar and cream, melt the chocolate, and add a little of the cream to it, so that it will be thin enough to pour in the remainder of the cream. Put the mixture in a pail with a tight cover, and set this inside a larger pail or pan. Beat the cream, with an egg-beater, until foamy. Fill the space between with pounded ice and rock-salt, using 3 c. ice to 1 c. salt. Turn the pail back and forth. Open occasionally, being careful that no salt falls in. Scrape the cream from the sides. Cover and turn again, and repeat this process until the cream is hard. It will freeze, usually, in 20 min.

STEAMED CUSTARD.

1 egg, 1 c. milk,
1 tbsp. sugar, spk salt, pinch nutmeg.

Beat slightly; add the other ingredients. Bake or steam in cups, from 10 to 20 min. Set in a pan of hot water and bake, or stand in a steamer over boiling water. Cook until a knife blade, when inserted, comes out clean.

BAKED OYSTERS.

3 tbsp. soft bread crumbs,
6 oysters, 1 level tsp. butter,
Salt, oyster liquor, or milk.

Melt the butter, and mix with the crumbs; season with salt. Cut the oysters in small pieces, sprinkle on the bottom of a buttered baking dish a little of the crumbs, then the oysters. Season; put the remainder of the cream on top. Moisten. Bake until the crumbs are brown.

TAPIOCA CREAM.

1 tbsp. pearl tapioca, 1 c. milk.
1 egg, pinch salt, 1-6 cup sugar.
¼ tsp. vanilla.

Pick over the tapioca, but in the top part of a double boiler, and cover with boiling water. As soon as the water is absorbed, add milk, and cook until the tapioca is soft and clear. Separate the egg, beat the yolk, add salt and sugar, pour on the hot milk, stirring as you pour. Cook until thick like soft custard. Beat the white stiff, and add, stir well. When cold, flavor.

ROASTED OYSTERS.

Take as many large oysters as are wished. Wash and dry them thoroughly with a clean towel; cut bacon in thin slices, put an oyster between two slices, and pin with wooden toothpicks. Roast until the bacon is crisp (very hot oven) and brown. Serve hot. Remove, or serve with, the toothpicks.

TOAST.

Cut stale bread in slices ½ in. thick, or in strips 1 in. wide. Lay the pieces on a wire toaster, and hold them at a little distance from the fire, turning often, so as to dry them well. Then hold nearer the fire, and toast on both sides until a golden brown.

BEEF JUICE, No. 2.

Scrape ½ lb. lean, juicy beef to a fine pulp. Put into a double boiler, with cold water in the lower part, and heat gradually, keeping it simmering 2 hrs., or until the meat is white. Strain, season when used. Serve hot.

IRISH MOSS JELLY.

½ c. Irish moss, 1 orange or lemon.

2 figs, ¼ c. sugar, 1 c. boiling water.

Pick over, wash, and soak the moss. Cut the figs in small pieces, pare the rind from the fruit. Place the rind, moss and figs in a sauce-pan, pour on the boiling water, stirring constantly, for 15 min., or until the liquid thickens. Add the fruit juice and sugar, stir until the sugar is dissolved, and press through a fine strainer into a cold wet mould. Set away to harden.

POTATO SOUP.

1 potato, ½ tsp. salt, ½ tsp. butter,

1 c. milk, ½ tsp. onion juice.

Wash and pare the potatoes. Cook until soft. Heat milk in double boiler, with onions. When the potato is done, mash, and thin with the milk. Rub through a strainer, and return to the boiler. Re-heat, add butter and salt, and tsp. chopped parsley if desired. Serve hot.

APPLE WATER.

Wipe a large sour apple, and without paring, cut into thin slices; put in a bowl and add strip lemon-peel, 1 tbsp. sugar, and 1 c. boiling water. Cover and set away to cool. Strain and serve with chipped ice.

TEA.

Heat a china or granite tea-pot by pouring in boiling water. Let it stand a moment, pour out the water, put in 1 tsp. tea, and 1 c. freshly boiling water. Set on the back part of the stove and steep 5 min. Never boil it.

HOW TO PREPARE AN ORANGE.

Take a firm, juicy orange, and with a sharp knife take off a thick paring, cutting through to the pulp. Cut out each section of pulp, being careful not to take any of the membranes. Remove the seeds and lay the sections on a pretty saucer. Sprinkle fine sugar over them, and small pieces of ice. Serve at once.

MACARONI SOUP.

1 c. stock, ¼ tsp. salt, 1 stick macaroni.

Cook the macaroni in boiling salted water about ½ hr., or until tender. Drain, and cut into small pieces; put into the stock; let come to a boil. Season. Serve hot.

BAKED APPLES.

Fill a small dish with apples, pared, quartered and sliced. Sprinkle on a little sugar, 1 tbsp. to each apple, and if very dry, add a little water. Baked, covered, until done, in a very moderate oven, ½ to 1 hr.

STEWED PRUNES.

Soak 1 c. prunes 2 or 3 hrs. Pour off the water in which they were soaked, cover with boiling water; simmer, closely covered, until tender. Add 2 tsp. sugar, and cook 3 min. longer. Set away to cool.

EGG VERMICELLI.

Separate the white from the yolk of 1 hard cooked egg. Chop fine, and mix with a little hot milk, or thin milk sauce. Season and pour over a slice of toast. Rub the yolk through a strainer over the top.

OMELET.

Separate 1 egg. To the yolk add a pinch salt; beat until creamy; then stir in 1 tbsp. milk. Beat the whites until stiff and fold into the yoke. Heat a small frying-pan. When hot, rub it around the edges with 1 tsp. butter, on a broad knife; let butter run all over the pan, and when bubbling, turn in the omelet. Set on a cool part of the stove until the albumen hardens underneath; then set in the oven on the grate until dry, and brown. Serve at once. A little chopped meat may be put into the yolks.

CRANBERRIES.

½ c. cranberries, ¼ c. cold water, ¼ c. sugar.

Pick over and wash the cranberries; put in a granite saucepan, with the cold water, closely covered. When they begin to boil, cook 5 min. Strain, or leave whole. Add sugar and cook 5 min longer. Pour into a mould, wet in cold water.

STEAMED RHUBARB.

½ c. rhubarb, ¼ c. sugar.

Wash the rhubarb and cut in inch-pieces; put in the top part of a double boiler; sprinkle over the sugar, and steam until soft. Do not stir.

STEAMED APPLES.

Wipe, core and pare the apples. Place in a steamer and cook until soft. Serve with cream and sugar, or rolled oats.

COFFEE.

1 hp. tbsp. coffee, 1 c. boiling water,
1 fresh egg shell.

Rinse out the coffee-pot with boiling water; put in the coffee, a little cold water, and the egg shell. Shake; add the freshly boiling water. Boil not longer than 5 min. Let stand on back of stove to settle,and pour down the spout a little cold water to clear away the grounds. Serve hot.

COCOA.

1 hp. tsp. cocoa, ½ c. milk,
½ c. boiling water, ½ tbsp. sugar.

Pour the water and milk into a sauce-pan, and add the sugar. Mix the cocoa to a smooth paste, with a little cold milk. When the liquid in the sauce-pan boils, stir in the cocoa, and let boil. Serve hot.

CHOCOLATE.

1 tbsp. chocolate, 1 c. milk,
1 tbsp. sugar, 1 tbsp. boiling water.

Scrape the chocolate, put it with the sugar and water in a sauce-pan, and stir over the fire until smooth and glossy. Scald the milk, and add to the chocolate. Let boil a moment and serve at once. Use more chocolate, if a richer drink is desired.

BAKED CRACKERS.

Butter plain, round crackers, and place them on a baking-tin. Set them on the grate of a hot oven, and bake 2 or 3 min., or until a golden brown. Watch them, to prevent burning. A little cheese may be sprinkled on each cracker, if desired.

FROZEN FRUIT.

1 large orange, ½ c. apricots,
1 large lemon, 1 c. sugar,
1 large banana, 1 c. cold water, or 1 c. cream.

Strain the juice of the orange and lemon into a bowl. Mash the remaining fruits through a fine strainer. Add the water to help in mashing, stir in sugar, and when dissolved, freeze. Use cream, if desired, or add ½ c. with the water.

BROILED CHOP OR STEAK.

Buy tender meat. Wipe and cut off all the fat. Grease a wire broiler with the fat, and lay in the meat. Hold over a clear fire, count ten slowly, turn, continue so until meat is done. If liked rare, 5 min. Well done, 10 min. Always have the meat ½ in. thick. Lay on a hot plate, season, add a small piece of butter and 1 tbsp. boiling water.

PAN-BROILED CHOP OR STEAK.

Use a frying-pan instead of a broiler. When it is hot, so that a little water, when thrown in, hisses, lay in the meat. Count and turn, the same as the Broiled Chop or Steak.

CORN-MEAL MUSH.

½ c. boiling water, ½ c. milk,
¼ c. corn-meal, pinch salt.

Put water on to boil. Mix the corn-meal, salt, and milk to a smooth paste. Pour on the boiling water, stir well, and boil about 20 min., stirring often. Serve hot, with cream and sugar. This mixture is delicious, if cooked in a double boiler from 1 to 1½ hrs.

MUFFINS, No. 1.

¾ c. flour, ½ tsp. Rumford baking powder,
½ c. milk, 1 egg, ½ tbsp. butter, melted.
Pinch salt.

Sift the dry ingredients into a bowl. Beat the egg. Pour in the milk, and stir gradually into the flour, to make a soft dough. Melt the butter, cool it, and stir into the dough. Fill greased gem pans 2-3 full, and bake in a moderate oven, 20 or 30 min. Try by a skewer, and when it comes out clean they are done.

CORN-MEAL GEMS.

2 level tbsp. yellow corn-meal,
4 level tbsp. flour, 2 level tbsp. sugar,
1 level tsp. baking powder, ½ c. milk,
Pinch salt, 1 level tsp. butter, melted.

Mix the same as for muffins; the sugar may be omitted. Graham or rye gems may be made by substituting the same amount of graham or rye meal, for the corn-meal.

SOFT-COOKED EGGS.

Put 1 pt. boiling water in a small sauce-pan. Let boil a moment, put an egg in it and remove from the fire. Let it stand 10 min., closely covered. The egg will then be soft and creamy.

PINEAPPLE SNOW.

⅛ box gelatine, 3 tbsp. cold water.
¾ c. pineapple, ½ c. sugar.
½ c. boiling water, juice ½ large lemon.
White 1 egg.

Soak the gelatine in the cold water ½ hr. Put the sugar, pineapple, and boiling water on to boil, simmer 10 min.; add the gelatine, and allow to remain over the fire until the gelatine is melted. Set away to cool. When it begins to thicken, add the lemon juice and the white, beaten stiff. Pour into a mould and set in a cool place to harden.

SPANISH CREAM.

Soak ¼ box gelatine in ½ c. cold milk ½ hr. Scald 1 c. milk in a double boiler; pour over gelatine, stir until dissolved. Beat the yolks of 2 eggs, and add to the gelatine; sweeten with 6 level tbsp. sugar. Return to the boiler and cook until it thickens, as for custard; beat whites until stiff, and pour custard over them. Mix well, flavor with ½ tsp. vanilla, and let harden in a mould.

SNOW CUSTARD.

Soak ½ box gelatine in ½ c. cold water, 1 hr. Dissolve by adding ½ c. boiling water; stir in 1 c. sugar, and ¼ c. lemon juice; strain; set away to cool. When it begins to stiffen, add the white of 1 large egg, beaten stiff, and beat until stiff enough to drop. Pour into a mould and set away to harden. Make a custard of the yolk of the egg, 1½ tbsp. sugar, pinch salt, 1 c. milk, and ½ tsp. vanilla. Flavor when cool. Serve with the snow.

CORNSTARCH. No. 1.

1 c. milk, ½ tbsp. cornstarch,
1 level tbsp. sugar, white 1 egg,
⅛ tsp. vanilla.

Blend the cornstarch in a little cold milk; dissolve the sugar in the hot milk; add the cornstarch and cook 10 min. When cool, add the beaten white and flavoring. A little melted chocolate may be added with the cornstarch.

RENNET.

1 c. new sweet milk,
1 tsp. liquid rennet,
1 tsp. sugar, pinch cinnamon.

Heat the milk until lukewarm. Dissolve the sugar in the milk; then add the rennet; sprinkle the cinnamon on top. Cool in a moderate heat, and when firm, put on ice. Do not let stand too long, or it will separate into curd and whey. If whey is desired for a drink, make it in this way. Stand a little longer and omit the sugar and cinnamon. Strain through muslin. Wine whey may be made by using white wine instead of rennet.

SOUR DRINK.

Put in a glass a tbsp. currant jelly and 1 tbsp. wine. Add enough ice water to fill the glass. Mix well. Serve cold. If the patient has very much fever, omit the wine.

MUTTON STEW.

½ lb. mutton, 1 tsp. carrot, cut fine,
1 c. cold water, 1 tsp. turnip, cut fine,
2 tsp. pearl barley, 1 tsp. minced parsley,
1 tsp. chopped onion, salt.

Remove all fat from the meat; if any bone, put the bone with the water into a sauce-pan, and simmer ½ hr. Cut the meat into cubes; put in a sauce-pan, with the barley (which should be thoroughly washed), and vegetables. Strain the water from the bones, pour over the meat and vegetables, and put where it will simmer, 1 hr. When it begins to bubble, skim. When done, add parsley. Cook 5 min. longer.

CORN COFFEE.

Roast an ear of corn until the tips of the kernels are black. Break the ear in pieces, and put in a bowl; then pour over it a pt. of boiling water. Stand until cold. Strain, and serve with broken ice in it.

CORNSTARCH, No. 2.

1 c. milk, scalded, ½ tbsp. cornstarch,
1 level tbsp. sugar, 1 small egg,
⅛ tsp. vanilla.

Blend the cornstarch in a little cold milk; dissolve the sugar in the hot milk; add cornstarch and cook 5 min. Remove from the fire, pour over the egg, which has been beaten; flavor; set away to cool.

CORNSTARCH BLANC MANGE.

1 c. milk, pinch salt,
2 level tbsp. cornstarch, 1 tbsp. sugar,
1 tbsp. grated chocolate.

Scald the milk in a double boiler. Mix the sugar, salt and chocolate in a very small sauce-pan; moisten with hot water, and stir over the fire until smooth and glossy; then add to the hot milk. Mix the cornstarch with a little cold milk; add to the other ingredients. Cook 10 min., until smooth and thick, stirring constantly. Then pour into moulds. Serve with cold cream and sugar.

FRUIT FOAM.

1 c. fresh fruit or berries.
White 1 egg, sugar.

Mash the fruit or berries and sweeten to taste. Add the beaten white; beat again, and set on ice. Serve very cold with cream.

MACARONI AND LAMB.

Cook ½ c. macaroni in boiling water 10 min.; drain. Cut ½ lb. lean lamb or mutton in small pieces. Cover with 1 pt. water, add macaroni, and cook until the meat is tender. Five min. before done, blend 1 level tbsp. flour with ¼ c. cream; pour into the lamb; season. Serve alone, or on toast.

CORN PONE.

1 c. corn-meal; 1 c. sour milk or cream; 1 egg (separate). ½ tbsp. butter and lard, pinch salt, ½ tsp. soda. Pour the milk into the corn-meal; stir until smooth. (Save out about ¼ c. of the milk to dissolve the soda in). Add yolk of egg, well beaten;

then soda. Mix well; then lard and butter, melted. Lastly, fold in the whites, beaten stiff. Bake in a shallow pan, 20 or 25 min.

CLARET PUNCH.

1 qt. claret, 1 c. whiskey,
Sugar to taste, 1 c. pineapple.

Dissolve the sugar in a little cold water; chop the pineapple, and mix all together. Set on ice at least for 2 hrs. Serve a portion of the pineapple with each glass.

CRACKER PANADA.

3 water crackers, 1 c. boiling water,
Pinch salt, 1 tbsp. sugar,
1 level tsp. butter.

Soften the crackers in the boiling water; sprinkle on the sugar and salt. Cut the butter in small pieces and put on top. Serve hot.

MUFFINS, No. 2.

1 c. flour, ½ tsp Rumford baking powder.
½ c. milk, white 1 egg.
½ tbsp. butter, melted, pinch salt.

Make the same as for Muffins, No. 1.

WHOLE WHEAT BREAD.

Dissolve 2 tsp. sugar and ¾ tsp. salt in 1 c. lukewarm milk; take ½ cake yeast and break into ½ c. lukewarm water; stir into the milk. Add whole wheat flour enough to make a stiff dough, 3 to 3½ c.; beat vigorously; then knead from 20 to 30 min. Put in a bowl, and set in a warm place for several hours. Then turn out on a board, using as little flour as possible, and knead 15 or 20 min. Shape into loaves or biscuits; put into greased pans; set in a warm place until double their bulk. If a loaf, bake from 50 min. to 1 hr.; if biscuits, a hotter oven, from 30 to 40 min.

GLUTEN GEMS.

Separate 2 eggs; beat the yolks until stiff and add to them 1 c. milk, 1 tbsp. melted butter, ½ tsp. salt, 1½ c. gluten flour, (into which 1 tsp. Rumford baking powder has been sifted), lastly, fold in the whites, beaten stiff. Bake in greased gem-pans, in a quick oven, 25 min.

BISCUIT WAFERS.

Rub 1 level tsp. butter and 1 c. flour to a fine powder. Add a small pinch of salt, and moisten with the white of 1 egg and a little milk, (do not beat the white), not too much, but so it can be handled. Lay on a floured board and beat with a rolling-pin from 20 to 30 min. Roll out, cut, and bake in a hot oven. Graham, oat-meal, or, in fact, any kind of biscuits, may be made by using the different flours.

WARMED-OVER RICE.

Thin cold cooked rice with beef, mutton or chicken stock. Put on the stove and cook until boiling hot. Mash through a fine sieve. Season with salt. Serve with a piece of buttered or dry toast.

FLOURED MILK, FOR CHILDREN.

Tie 1 c. flour in a bag and boil hard for 10 hrs. Take out of the bag, and dry in a moderate oven. Take 1 tbsp. of the flour and thin with 1 c. cold milk. Give to a child with a soda cracker.

SNOW PUDDING.

2 tbsp. gelatine, yolk 1 large egg.
2 tbsp. cold water, 1½ tbsp. sugar.
½ c. boiling water, pinch salt.
½ c. sugar, 1 c. milk.
2 tbsp. orange juice, ½ tsp. vanilla.
1 tsp. wine, white 1 large egg.

Soak the gelatine in the cold water 30 min., or until soft; add the boiling water, sugar, orange juice and wine; stir until the sugar is dissolved. Strain into a bowl and set in ice water to cool. Stir occasionally. Beat the white of egg to stiff froth, and when the gelatine begins to stiffen, add the white and beat all together until very light. When nearly stiff enough to drop, pour into a mould. Do not add the white of egg too soon, or it will require so much more time to beat. 10 or 15 min. should be sufficient. Make a custard of the other ingredients, and serve with the snow. Pour the sauce around the snow, not over it. Set the snow on ice several hours before serving.

ORANGE BASKETS.

Cut as many oranges as will be required, leaving peel whole for the baskets, and a strip half an inch wide the handle. Remove the pulp and juice and use the juice in making orange jelly, or snow pudding. Place the baskets in a pan of broken ice to keep upright. Fill with orange jelly, or, in fact, any jelly or pudding. When ready to serve, put a spoonful of whipped cream in each basket. Serve in a bed of green leaves.

RHUBARB JELLY.

Soak 1 tbsp. gelatine in ½ c. cold water, ½ hr. Take ½ lb. rhubarb, make a syrup with ½ c. sugar. To this add the rhubarb, cut in small pieces. Cook until tender, in a double boiler. Add the juice of 2 lemons, and the dissolved gelatine. Pour into a mould. Set away to harden.

CALVES'-FOOT JELLY.

Soak ½ box gelatine in 1 c. cold water until the gelatine is soft; then add 1 c. boiling water in which the thin rind of 1 lemon has been boiled. Then add the juice of the lemon, 1 c. sugar and ¾ c. port wine. When cool, pour into jars; seal. When wanted for use, set the jar on ice until the jelly is firm.

ORANGE CREAM.

Soak 2 tbsp. gelatine in ¼ c. cold water, ½ hr. Dissolve in 1 c. boiling water. Add the juice of 2 oranges, and 1 tbsp. sugar. When it begins to harden, beat in 4 tbsp. of whipped cream. Pour into a mould and set on ice until hard. This orange cream may be served in orange baskets.

RASPBERRY CREAM.

Soak 2 tbsp. gelatine in ½ c. cold water, ½ hr. Boil together ½ c. milk and ½ c. cream, and sweeten to taste. Dissolve gelatine in the boiling liquid (be sure and heat the cream and milk in a double boiler), return to the boiler and let remain on the stove about 3 or 4 min. Add 3 tbsp. of fruit juice, or if you use raspberry jelly, omit the sugar. Put into a pan; set in water and beat until it begins to thicken. Pour into a mould; set in a cold place. Serve surrounded with whipped cream. Any kind of fruit juice may be used.

EGG GRUEL.

Beat the yolk of 1 egg with 1 tbsp. white sugar. Pour 1 c. boiling milk on it. Add the white of the egg, beaten stiff. Season with a pinch of spice.

RYE MUSH.

Take 4 tbsp. of rye flour, mix smooth with a little water, and stir it into 2 c. of boiling water; boil 20 min., stirring frequently. To be eaten with cream or milk and sugar.

GLUTEN MUSH.

½ c. gluten, 1 c. boiling water, ½ tsp. salt.

Mix the gluten and salt together. Stir this gradually into the boiling water. Cook ½ hr. in a double boiler, stirring often.

RICE WATER.

2 tbsp. rice, 1 qt. cold water
Salt and sugar to taste.

Pick over and wash the rice, and cook in the water, or until the rice is very soft. Add salt and sugar. If you wish to use it as a jelly, add a little lemon juice, not too much, and mash through a fine sieve into a mould. When cold, it may be served with sugar and cream. This may also be made into a drink, but it will require more hot water, so it will be a thin liquid, and of course it must boil longer. If used as a drink, add a little spice. Stick cinnamon is a great improvement. It can easily be removed.

BARLEY SOUP.

Cut 1 lb. of mutton into small pieces and put into 1 pt. cold water, with 1 tbsp. barley. Heat slowly, and simmer 2 hrs. Skim, season, and serve hot.

SLIPPERY ELM TEA.

Pour 1 c. boiling water upon 1 tsp. of slippery-elm powder, or a piece of the bark. When cool, strain and flavor with lemon juice and sugar.

BAKED LEMONS.

Bake sour lemons or oranges 20 min. in a moderate oven. When done, open at once and take out the inside. Sweeten with sugar. This is excellent for hoarseness.

VINEGAR SYRUP.

Take 1 c. vinegar, ½ c. sugar and 2 tbsp. butter. Cook until it has become a syrup. This is excellent for a cough or hoarseness. Keep in or near a warm place.

BAKED ONIONS.

Take a large onion, and bake until soft; then eat; or put sugar on the same, as for baked lemons. Sliced onions are good to put on the chest for soreness.

Vegetables to Serve with Meats.

ROAST BEEF—Roast potatoes, Yorkshire pudding, stewed celery and baked tomatoes.

ROAST VEAL—Roast parsnips or parsnip fritters, mashed potatoes and lettuce.

ROAST PORK—Sweet potatoes, apple sauce and turnips.

ROAST LAMB—Mint or currant jelly sauce, potato puff, macaroni and cheese, and spinach.

CHICKEN—Stewed cauliflower, creamed potatoes, asparagus and sliced tomatoes.

LAMB CHOPS—Sauce, peas, potato chips, and spinach on toast.

FRIED OYSTERS—Peas, French fried potatoes and cold slaw.

TURKEY—Stewed onions, cranberries, mashed potatoes, scalloped oysters and corn.

ROAST DUCK—Apple sauce, mashed potatoes, raw oysters, and scalloped onions.

ROAST GOOSE—Mashed potatoes, stewed onions, sauer kraut and apple sauce.

VENISON—Lyonnaise potatoes, currant jelly, steamed rice and mashed turnips.

MENUS.

DINNER.

Tomato Soup, Croutons,
Baked Fish, mushroom sauce, Potato Balls,
Lobster Salad, Crackers.
Oyster Patties,
"Breaded Lamb Chops, Peas, Sliced Tomatoes, Mayonnaise
Bread and Butter,"
Welsh Rarebit.
Ice Cream, — Cake,
Coffee.

DINNER.

Soup, Cracker or Croutons,
Fried Chicken, Cauliflower,
Creamed Potatoes, Asparagus,
Sliced Tomatoes, Mayonnaise,
Snow Custard, Small Cakes.
Coffee.

DINNER.

Soup.
Veal Croquettes, Peas, Bread and Butter,
Potato Chips, Stewed Onions,
Tomato Salad, Crackers.
Spanish Cream, Pound Cake,
Tea, Coffee.

SUPPER.

Veal Loaf, Sliced Tomatoes,
Muffins, Prunes.
Float, Love Cakes,
Chocolate.

SUPPER.

Cold Roast Meat,
Bread, Preserves.

Potato Salad,   Stuffed Eggs,
Tapioca Cream,
Tea or Chocolate.

SUPPER.

Scalloped Meat,
Rolls,   Lettuce,   Dressing.
Baked Apples and Cream,
Tea or Coffee.

SUPPER.

Stewed Oysters,   Crackers,
Foamy Omelet,   Bread,
Cup Custards.   Ginger Bread,
Chocolate.

LUNCHEON.

Meat Omelet   Hot Biscuits,
Toast,   Coffee.

LUNCHEON.

Scalloped Salmon,   Creamed Potatoes,
Bread,   Chocolate,
Apple Whip.

LUNCHEON.

Fried Oysters,   Tomato Salad, No. 1,
Brown Bread,   Pickles,
Milk.

LUNCHEON.

Broiled Fish,   Crackers,
Sliced Tomatoes,   Rolls,
Sponge Cake.   Fruit,
Chocolate.

LUNCHEON.

Deviled Crabs.
Bread,   Cold Slaw,
Strawberry Whip.

BREAKFAST.

Fruit,
Rolled Oats,   Cream and Sugar,
Broiled Steak,
French Fried Potatoes,   Omelet,
Muffins,   Coffee.

BREAKFAST.

Mush,
Stewed Kidney,   Fried Sweet Potatoes,
Rolls,   Cocoa.

BREAKFAST.

Oatmeal,
Pan Broiled Chops,   Baked Eggs,
Hashed Browned Potatoes,
Graham Muffins.
Griddle Cakes,   Caramel Syrup.

BREAKFAST.

Cream of Wheat,
Fried Ham,   Meat Omelet,
Sliced Tomatoes,   Toast,
Chocolate.

How and When to do Things.

WHEN TO SERVE OLIVES.

Olives are served at luncheons, dinners and suppers. They should be on the table before the meal is announced. Serve them on broken ice in a pretty dish.

HOW TO SERVE SARDINES.

Sardine plates may be used. If you have none, any kind of a pretty plate may be used. Drain the oil from the fish, and place them on the plate. Garnish with slices of lemon.

HOW TO ROLL BREAD.

Cut bread into slices; remove crusts; spread thinly with butter. Roll up carefully, having the butter side inward, and lay on a napkin. Keep moist by rolling bread in the napkin, and pin. A small piece of lettuce may be rolled in the bread. Rolled bread is nice to serve with raw oysters, sardines, or at supper, luncheon, and picnics.

HOW TO MAKE MERINGUES.

Meringues are made to put on pies, puddings, etc. It is a French word, and means "whites of eggs beaten stiff with sugar." Remember meringues should be baked in a moderate oven, and that pulverized sugar should be used.

GELATINE.

Always soak gelatine by putting on enough cold water to cover it, and let stand a certain length of time. Dissolve by pouring boiling water over it.

HOW TO MAKE CARAMEL.

Put the amount of sugar desired in a frying-pan, stir over the fire until the sugar is melted and browned. Now add hot water equal in quantity to the sugar, and let the mixture simmer until all the sugar is dissolved. It should become perfectly liquid, but be careful and not cook too long, or it will harden. Caramel is used in mousses, soups, sauces, etc.

HOW TO DRY PARSLEY.

Wash parsley and lay in a moderate oven until perfectly dry; then crumble and keep in a tin box. Or, you can dry parsley by letting it lie in the sun until perfectly dry. This is a good way to fix parsley for soups, sauces, etc.

HOW TO MAKE VEGETABLE BALLS.

Much depends on the manner in which the vegetable is cut. They may be cut in dice, cubes, etc., or if you can purchase vegetable scoops, do so, and you will find that the vegetables are much prettier.

HOW TO WASH BUTTER.

Rinse a bowl in boiling water, and then in cold water. Put a piece of butter into the bowl, and after covering it with cold water, work it with the hands, until all the salt has been washed out. Pour off the water, and press out any particles that may remain in the butter.

HOW TO PACK A FREEZER.

For 1 gal. freezer, use 4 c. rock salt. Put in a layer of ice, then salt; continue so doing until the freezer is packed within 2 in. from the top. Then wipe carefully, for fear some of the salt might get into the can.

Always rinse can with cold water, and put into firkin before putting in the mixture, so in case there should be anything wrong it could easily be attended to.

Always have the mixture ready before you break the ice. Have a bag made of ticking, also have a hammer. Break the ice in small pieces.

Never mix the salt and ice together before putting into the freezer.

The less salt you can use, and make the cream firm, the better the cream.

Turn the freezer slowly the first ten minutes, (or you might make butter), then rapidly the next ten minutes. If you use the "Gem Ice Cream Freezer," it will take only twenty minutes to make the cream.

Do not fill the can too full, as it expands while freezing.

After the cream is frozen enough, remove dasher, beat hard for three or four minutes; then put a piece of white paper over can, (this prevents the air from getting in, also any salt), put on lid; press down tight; sprinkle ice and salt over top; cover with a piece of carpet; set in a cool place (cellar) until ready for use. At serving time, remove ice about 3 in. from top of can, wipe carefully, dip spoon in lukewarm water and put on plates that have been on ice for several hours. Dip spoon each time before helping the plate.

The Table and Serving.

Table cloths should be laid without wrinkles and perfectly straight.

The sharp edge of knives should be turned towards the plate.

Bowls of spoons and tines of forks must be turned up.

Place the knives, soup spoons, butter plate and tumblers at the right of the plate. If bread and butter plates are used, place at the left; also the bone dishes.

Place the forks and napkins at the left of the plate.

Put the knife and fork six or seven inches apart.

If there is nothing in the center of the knife and fork, the napkin may be placed there.

Place the small spoon in front of the plate.

Do not place tablespoons crossed on the table. Place one in front of each tureen.

Serve sliced tomatoes on a steak platter; serve with a fork.

Butter must not be put on the table too soon, as it will become soft and oily.

Bread should be freshly cut. Do not put the bread on in whole slices. Cut in halves.

Water must be fresh and cool, and only fill the glasses three-fourths full. Glasses must be kept filled.

Everything for one course must be removed before serving another.

In clearing a table, the food must be removed first; then the soiled dishes; then clean dishes, and lastly the crumbs.

Remove soiled dishes from the right; also remember, if you are to place anything on the table yourself, go to the right.

Always go to the left when a person is to take anything from the tray.

Olives and pickles may be served with forks, if you have no olive or pickle fork, use your fingers.

In eating olives and pickles, never cut them; take them up with the fingers.

Never take bread from the plate with the fork.

Never spread a piece of bread at one time; break and spread as wanted.

Allow bread to rest partly on the plate, and partly on the table.

Always lay biscuits on plate, as they are greasy and will soil the table cloth.

Remember, the teaspoon should never be left in the cup.

Always use finger-bowls, especially in fruit season, as there is nothing that will ruin the linen as readily as fruit juice.

Have a small pitcher of hot water to rinse the cups well before pouring in the beverage.

Do not pile your soiled dishes on your plate. The one serving removes them.

Never fold napkin unless napkin ring is at the place. Be sure and put in ring; if not, simply catch it in the center of napkin, and lay it at the left hand side of your place.

Do not put plates around at places. Stand in a pile at the right hand of the carver; then he can put one in front, help, and hand with his right hand to server.

Never remove knife and fork when passing plate for second serving; place carefully to one side.

Serve jelly on a pretty plate, not in the glass.

Salads may be served in a salad dish, or piled in a mound in the center of a steak platter. Pour mayonnaise dressing over and around, garnish with slices of hard cooked eggs.

Another way to serve salad is to arrange small curly lettuce leaves in groups of three, and place 1 tbsp. of the salad mixture in the center of the cup thus formed; or one medium-sized leaf may be used. Serve with a tbsp. mayonnaise, or any salad dressing, on top.

Rumford
BAKING POWDER.

It is different from and superior to **all** other powders, giving better results in baking than the best of them, and **will retain its strength indefinitely in any climate.**

It produces the finest cake, biscuit, muffins, etc., which will retain their fresh condition longer than those made with any other powder, and imparts no bitter or other disagreeable baking-powder-taste to the food.

Miss Kate Edna Negley, Teacher of Cooking, Central Board of Education, Pittsburg, says:

"I have given Rumford Baking Powder a thorough trial, and find it very satisfactory indeed. In fact it is one of the best powders I have ever used."

The price is much less than other high-grade powders, because of recent improvements in the manufacture.

15 cts. half pound can.
30 cts. one pound can.

Our Shoes

ARE OF THE

Highest Grade.

Our Prices among the Lowest.
Our Stock the Largest in the East End.

Our Specialties: Shoes for the Boys and Girls, the best made; Ladies $3 and $4 Grades.

First Class Shoe Repairing.

Geo. H. Stoebener,

{ 6227 Penn Avenue,
{ 22 Frankstown Avenue.

Phone 140, E.E.

A. E SPAHR,

Successor to

W. J. SPAHR,

GROCER.

Vegetables, Poultry, Butter and Eggs.

Table Water, Ginger Ale and Root Beer,

6117 Penn Avenue, East End.

Telephone, E. E. 47.

The Way

To reach a man's heart is through his stomach. A Box of

Upstill's Cigars

Will reach further.

Finest Line in E. E.

141 S. Highland Ave.

Kissner's

Home-made Candies,

Fresh Every Day.

CHOCOLATES,
BON BONS
AND
TAFFIES.

6103 Penn Ave.,   95 Federal St.,
East End.   Allegheny
Telephone 82 E.E.

We are already established, and doing business. We most cordially invite one and all to visit us at once; get familiar with our system of business, and avail yourselves of the conveniences and advantages we offer. In shopping the careful housewife will do well to examine our stock of latest goods in all lines and compare with prices elsewhere.

Your interests are identical with ours, therefore you should share the benefit, as a visit to our store will amply repay you.

Mail and Telephone orders have our prompt and careful attention.

PENN AND HIGHLAND AVENUES.

Yours Very Respectfully,

C. H. ROWE & CO.

SIMPSON & CO.,

Provisions.

Fresh and Smoked Meats.

Good Goods.

—o—

FISH AND OYSTERS.

—o—

Fair Prices.

Butter, Eggs, Poultry.

6021 Penn Avenue.

Telephone E. E. 178.

Pillsbury's Best

and

Pillsbury's Vitos,

The Best Family Flour

AND THE FINEST

BREAKFAST FOOD.

S. EWART & CO.,

921, 923, 925 LIBERTY ST.

Our Aim

Is constantly seeking to secure the BEST GOODS for the value and to give satisfaction to our customers. We handle the

Pilgrim Brand of Canned Goods

AND

California Fruits, Princess Extracts, Etc.

Vegetables and Fruits in Season

George Welfer,

Groceries and Produce,

606 Homewood Avenue, East End.

Headquarters

FOR

Kitchen Novelties, Refrigerators, Ice Cream Freezers and Bird Cages.

Edward Acker,

132 S. Hiland Ave., E. E.

Tel. 56 E. E.

Vincent, Scott & Co.,

6023 Penn Avenue.

—:o:—

FINE CARPETS AND FURNITURE, STEAM CARPET CLEANING.

Furniture Repairing,
Awnings Made to Order.

Telephone E. E. 81.

R. D. Brent,

Apothecary,

Penn and Highland Avenues.

Prices as low as consistent with the use of finest Drugs.

Decorations

for all

Occasions.

Cut Flowers our Specialty.

B. F. Becker & Co.,

FLORISTS,

6105 Penn Avenue,

EAST END   -   PITTSBURG, PA.

Telephone E. E. 190.

LOUIS KABLE,

Ladies' Tailoring,

118 Collins Avenue,

EAST END - - - PITTSBURG.

Telephone 145.

THE LEADING

DRY GOODS STORE

in the

EAST END

IS

Mansmann's,

Penn and Collins.

Demmler Bros.,

LEADING

Kitchen Furnishers,
Alaska Refrigerators.

Peerless Steam Cookers,

Silverware, Cutlery, Chafing Dishes,
5 O'clock Tea Kettles, Gas
Ranges.

Oil And Gasoline Stoves.

GLOBE WASHER MAKES WASHDAY EASY.

Gilroy's Patent
Curtain Stretchers.

Pasteur Water Filters.

All the latest and best inventions for the Kitchen.

Demmler Bros.,
526-8 Smithfield Street,
PITTSBURG, PA.

THE NEGLEY COOK BOOK.

Ritter's Concentrated Unfermented GRAPE JUICE is absolutely Pure and is the best article of the kind either for the Sick or for use as a Healthful Beverage.

Ritter's Salad Dressing, Salad Oil.

Tomato Catsup, Pure German Mustard, and Pure Fruit Syrups (the last for use in Sherberts, Ices, Ice Cream, and in place of Wine Sauce for Puddings), are articles which need only to be tried to be appreciated.

PHILIP J. RITTER CONSERVE CO.,
Philadelphia, Pa.

ALBERT J. THRASHER,
Sole Agent for Pittsburg, Pa.

THE OHIO MAPLE SYRUP CO.,
Burton, Geauga County, O.,

Is located in the County which produces the most and the Finest Maple Syrup of any County in the United States.

This Syrup will be found mentioned upon the menu of the Waldorf-Astoria Hotel of New York, and can be had upon the tables of many other of the finest hotels in the United States.

•

People are beginning to learn that

L. A. BENEDICT & SON'S
QUAKER • BRAND

Of Evaporated Corn, when properly cooked, is a most economical and palitable food. One package will go as far as two cans of corn.

The supply has never yet been equal to the demand.

ALBERT J. THRASHER,
PITTSBURG, PA.

Sole Agent for States East of Ohio.

Everything Beautiful

And everything new will be found in our stock. We are headquarters for **WEDDING AND ANNIVERSARY PRESENTS**, and everything in the line of household necessities in the line of Crockery.

CHINA Dinner Sets, Tea Sets, After dinner Sets, Chocolate Sets, Ice Cream Sets, etc.

CUT GLASS Berry Dishes, Water Pitchers, Water Bottles, Tumblers, Glasses, Sugars, Salts, Flower Vases etc.

LAMPS, Onyx and Gold, China, Metal, Dresden, Rockwood, etc. Globes and Shades to Match.

ART POTTERY, Bric-a-Brac, Onyx Stands, Onyx Cabinets, etc.

All the Rich Royal Wares Prices Are Very Low. Our Name Guarantees Quality.

T. G. EVANS & CO.,
235 Fifth Ave., Pittsburg.

A. BRADLEY & CO.,
200-202 Wood St.,
Pittsburg, Pa.

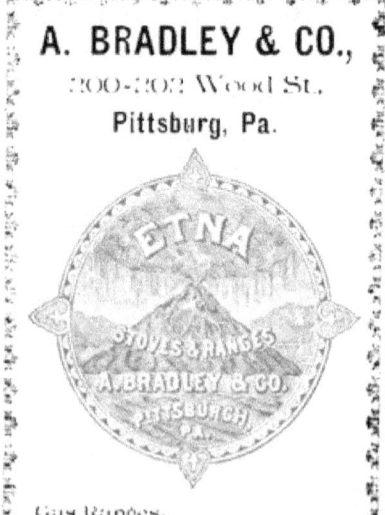

Gas Ranges.
Gas Stoves.
Kensington Furnaces.

W. C. MOHLER,
PRACTICAL PLUMBER AND GAS FITTER.
5606 Penn Avenue, near Negley,
EAST END, PITTSBURG.
Telephone E. E. 222.

D. J. Kennedy,

Dealer in

Anthracite and Bituminous Coal and Coke,

Fine Front Brick,

Lime, Sand, Cements, Sewer Pipes and Fire Brick,

Acme Wall Plaster,

150 Frankstown Ave.,
EAST END. PITTSBURG.
Telephone 529 E. E.

Campbell & Slocum,

Plate,

Window

and

Stained Glass,

805 Liberty Avenue,
Pittsburg, Pa.

Telephone 1895.

Goehring, Curll & Bartley,

FINE BUILDERS' HARDWARE,
PAINTERS' SUPPLIES,
HOUSEFURNISHING GOODS,
WINDOW and PLATE GLASS.

6203 PENN AVENUE,
PITTSBURG, PA.

'Phone 341 E. E.

THE NEGLEY COOK BOOK.

"Peerless"

NON-ALCOHOLIC

FLAVORING POWDERS.

—FOR FLAVORING—

Ice Cream, Water Ices, Cakes, Candies, Custards, Etc.,
In the following Flavors:

Orange,	Lemon,	Strawberry,	Wintergreen,
Vanilla,	Celery,	Rose,	Almond,
Peppermint,	Nutmeg,	J. Ginger,	Strawberry,

Superior to the liquid extracts in Delicacy and Richness of Flavor. The very best Flavorings that can be produced.

ABSOLUTELY PURE.

The American Journal of Health, New York, in an endorsement of our goods, March 10th, 1898, says:—

"Peerless Flavoring Powders have stood the strongest tests, and for that reason solely do we fully endorse them and unhesitatingly place them among food products worthy of the patronage of the most careful house-keepers."

Put up in 2½ ounce boxes; price 25 cents per box, by mail, prepaid, or of our agents.

—NOT SOLD IN STORES.—
——RESIDENT AGENTS WANTED.

OLIVER C. MacKALIP,

Station D, PITTSBURG, PA.

Sole Manufacturers and Proprietors.

GEO. R. Mathieu,
Electrical Contractor,

Dealer in Electrical Supplies.

OFFICE: 508 N. HIGHLAND AVENUE or 6000 HOEVELER ST., PITTSBURG, PA.

EAST END.

ESTIMATES FURNISHED.

Every Kind Of Electrical Construction and Repair Work Promptly Attended to.

Telephone 172 E. E.

F. W. Sawert.   J. H. Sawert.

F. W. SAWERT & CO.,
Carriage Builders,

OFFICE AND REPOSITORIES:

Nos. 5917, 5919, 5921 and 5923 Penn Ave.

Factory. 5916, 5918, 5920 & 5922 Kirkwood St.

Pittsburg, Pa.

Repairing Neatly and Promptly Executed

M. F. Petrwosky,

DEALER IN

Wall Paper, Room Mouldings, Etc.

Pictures Framed to Order.

NO. 111 SHERIDAN AVE.,

East End.

We can always put our hands on the shoes you want in two minutes—we've got 000 sorts, and know where they are.

To do this, we've got to keep stock clear of old styles and odds and ends. We do it by selling for half to two-thirds.

Come for the offerings, 20 or 30 sorts of shoes for half to two-thirds.

W. M. LAIRD.

400 to 440 Market St.

Pittsburg, Pa.

Anything in

HIGH CLASS COOKERY.

Can be obtained at the

Catering House

of

W. R. KUHN & CO.,

6202 Penn Avenue.

'Phone 158. 679 E. E.

In MEDICINES QUALITY is of the FIRST IMPORTANCE.

James Kerr, Jr.,

Apothecary,

Corner Center and Highland Avenues,

PITTSBURG, PA.

Telephone J E.E.

Jos. Eichbaum & Co.,

PRINTERS, STATIONERS, BLANK BOOK MAKERS,

Steel and Copper Plate Engravers and Printers.

Fancy Goods, Artists' Materials, The "CALIGRAPH"

Type Writer, Type Writer Supplies.

242 Fifth Avenue,

PITTSBURG, PA.

Jarrett Bros.,

HOME PORTRAIT ARTISTS.

BEAUTIFUL EFFECT

AND

MORE NATURAL EXPRESSION

OBTAINED IN YOUR OWN HOMES.

6200 Penn Avenue.

Phone 721 E. E.

PHOTOGRAPHIC STUDIO,

6117 Penn Avenue,

East End, Pittsburg.

(Established 1877.)

High ART PHOTOGRAPHS and CARBONETS a speciality.

Pictures enlarged and executed in fine PASTEL CRAYON.

Give us a call and we will surely satisfy you.

FREDRICK & FULTON.

Fashionable

Tailors,

6004 Penn Avenue,

East End, - - Pittsburg, Pa.

Phone 613 E. E.

J. H. FREDRICK, CUTTER.

GRAFF & COMPANY.

GRAFTON STOVES, RANGES AND FURNACES.

Mantels and Tiling.

917 Liberty Street, Pittsburg, Pa.

Jewel Grafton Drop Oven Door Ranges.

THE NEGLEY COOK BOOK.

R. M. Sterrett,

Druggist,

6130 Penn Avenue,

Pittsburg, Pa.

Drugs, Spices, Flavorings, Extracts,

Perfumery and Fancy Toilet Articles.

Physicians' Prescriptions a Specialty.

Telephone E. E. 239.

HIGH GRADE FOOTWEAR.

Never in the history of our store have we been able to offer such an elegant line of Footwear to our patrons as this season. It has been selected with the utmost care, and with a view of pleasing the most particular dressers.

All the newest effects in Tans, Patent Leather, for Ladies, Misses and Children.

Fine Footwear for Men always a specialty with us,

JOHN H. WATT,

6005 Penn Avenue,

EAST END.   PITTSBURG, PA.

PHONE 251-3 E E.

Attract Attention.

Our Shoes do, because they are Dressy and Look Well. We always have the Latest Styles from the best manufacturers.

Special: Ladies' Fine Shoes from $2.15 to $3.50.

Ludebuehl's

3 Franktown Ave, E. E.

E. W. HAGAN,

243-5 5th Avenue,

Pittsburg, Pa.,

Caterer.

Estimates for every Requisite for Weddings, Dinners and Receptions.

Cafe Open After the Theater.

SHOPPERS' QUICK LUNCH.

Groceries.

A complete stock of reliable eatables at moderate prices is what makes our business grow.

Vegetables

Fresh and tasty—gathered in the early morning—here for your picking daily. Every day is market day here.

Poultry.

Cleaned here on the premises assures tender, fresh and wholesome poultry to our trade.

Chinaware

Lastly, on which to eat all the good things this store affords housewives. A complete selection upstairs; prices surprisingly reasonable. Visit the store of

KUHN & BRO.,
LEADING GROCERS OF THE EAST END.
6113-15 Penn Ave.
Telephone 1889.

GEO. K. STEVENSON & CO.,
GROCERS,

We have a tempting array of good things at tempting prices. We particularly invite all who are not familiar with our stores, to visit either or both, and see how attractive food stores can be made.

We have always felt that a Grocery Store should be made inviting, and have endeavored to make ours so, not only in the display of goods, but in prices as well.

GEO. K. STEVENSON & CO.,
STORES; Sixth Ave., opp. Trinity Church.
TWO { Center & Highland Aves., E. E.
Pittsburg, Pa.

The Most Delicious.

MacDonald's

CANDIES

and

Ice Cream Soda.

Reception and Luncheon Candies,

Flavors, etc.,

208 Sixth Street,

Pittsburg, Pa.

CUT GLASS.

SIEDLE,

JEWELER-SILVERSMITH

East End.

STERLING SILVER.

ART GOODS.

DIAMONDS.

Recipe for High Grade Printing.

As many words as necessary, four or five styles of good, plain "TYPE." Proper quality and quantity of "Paper," printed carefully on a good "Press," add skill of "Compositor" and artistic taste of "Pressman."

These ingredients, properly handled, will make the most satisfactory "dish" for the progressive merchant.

Be careful not to let it stand until it gets too cold—This is best served hot—red hot.

The Index,

Stevenson Building.

East End.   -   -   -   -   PITTSBURG, PA.

Telephone 619 E. E.

www.ingramcontent.com/pod-product-compliance
Lightning Source LLC
Chambersburg PA
CBHW020840160426
43192CB00007B/729